The
EMERGING DANIEL COMPANY

Aaron Evans

INTRODUCTION

A company of people is emerging that will have spiritual understanding, sensitivity, and courage to receive the kingdom in this present age and the age to come. They will affect and influence those who are called to the "seven mountains of cultural influence" with the seven spirits of God: wisdom, understanding, counsel, knowledge, might, the Spirit of the Lord, and the Spirit of the fear of the Lord.

This book relates the understanding and protocol that is needed to transition and cooperate in the restoration of this biblical apostolic promise. This book will also convey insight that will help identify and equip this Emerging Daniel Company for the *emergency* of the last days with understanding, structure, life, and impartation. Daniel 2:21 says that knowledge is given to those who have an understanding heart. We must seek it, pray for it, and set our hearts for it (Daniel 10:12) using Daniel as a prototype or pattern. We must move in 4D— the fourth dimension of devotion, discovery, development, and deployment.

Understanding is the real-time comprehension of what works and why. It is the spirit of understanding the *why* that can be imparted so that others can receive life-changing direction during difficult and transitional times. Understanding is seeing behind-the-scenes.

Living a life with understanding comes from a lifestyle that is devoted to the Lord, His ways, and His presence. Transformational truths for understanding the times and how to prepare, empowers us to be fruitful in this season of the Spirit.

We must submit ourselves to corporate intercession for understanding in order to cooperate with heaven's purpose. As Daniel was, we want to be "the wise who shine" (Daniel 12:3) and the wise who understand (Daniel 12:9-10).

As you examine this book and engage the revelation it contains, may the Spirit of wisdom and understanding come and rest upon you. We really are in the kingdom for such a time as this—participants in a kingdom reformation which is being orchestrated by the Lord of Hosts.

The days of light and darkness are intensifying. Let us shine for our light has come and the glory of the Lord is upon us.

Aaron Evans
THE EMERGING DANIEL
COMPANY INTERNATIONAL

ACKNOWLEDGMENT

I am deeply grateful to so many who have helped make this book possible. This book has taken over twenty years of personal preparation and five years to write. I am convinced beyond a shadow of doubt that everyone that contributed was divinely sent into my life to see that it was accomplished.

Special thanks to the many that helped to edit this book from beginning to end with research, typing, transcribing and encouragement: Jordan Bateman, Michele Gunn, Lauren Stinton, Deb Williams, Diane Hartman, Cal Beverly and my amazing wife, Jill-Marie.

My wife and son Josiah will receive a great reward from the Lord just because of their patience and understanding during this time.

To all the spiritual mentors that helped shape my life and to all those who have and are walking with Jill-Marie and myself, we honor you before God and man.

Last, but certainly not least, my deepest appreciation for the Holy Spirit's guidance in inspiring, revealing, illuminating and for the timing of the release of the words that follow.

FOREWORD

Aaron Evans has been a personal friend for more than 15 years. I have watched with great appreciation as God has developed his character, expanded his understanding and supernaturally groomed him for a vital end-of-the-age task that he is uniquely qualified to fulfill. Through the years I have watched and marveled as God strategically placed Aaron in various places and ministries in order to extract from each certain spiritual DNA that has now been mingled into a ministry that will cross all barriers and touch every culture, background and tradition.

Aaron's book, "the Emerging Daniel Company" is more than a compilation of revelatory insight and words of wisdom captured through those years of preparation. Instead, it functions more as a divine invitation into a journey with God that has been long prophesied and immensely needed.

Going back as far as the patriarch Enoch we have discovered this cherished position of friendship with God and walking with Him in intimacy, fellowship and power. The book that you hold in your hand will unlock biblical mysteries and sound wisdom to facilitate that reality and awaken holy desire to know the Lord fully.

The Bible describes that a great "cloud of witnesses" surrounds us with the hope of us obtaining this promise so that they will be made perfect. (See Hebrews 11:39-40) Each of these champions represents a token company of people that saw something prophetically and gave their lives for its fulfillment. Although the Bible tells us this group did not fully achieve that promise, the Scripture emphasizes that an end-time company of people will find this place in God to become His "dwelling place."

When this occurs, the Bible tells us that those who have sown and those who reap this cherished promise will rejoice together in a grand union of both the old and the new. "The Emerging Daniel Company" is saturated with nuggets of wisdom to help facilitate this reality and initiate the great harvest. Most assuredly, the prophet Daniel will rejoice when the end-time "Daniel Company" walks in the promises he foresaw.

Many years ago the Lord told me that Daniel was a prototype of the generation he foresaw. This notable prophet was a man of integrity and revelation who understood the spiritual realm and how to live in it. He was entrusted with such fantastic insight into God's plan of victory that they were concealed until the time of their application. The Bible plainly states that he saw the end-of-the-age generation that would possess the mysteries of God's Kingdom and release them in the Earth. This would cause them to be so illuminated that they would shine like the brightness of the expanse of Heaven and lead many to righteousness in a grand fulfillment of promise and a harvest of the ages.

With integrity and sound interpretive skills, Aaron Evans has captured that prophetic promise and begun the process of preparing a company of people to live as those who overcome the spirit of this age and all opposition to fully achieve divine destiny. They will be identified as the end-time champions who possess the nature and ability of Christ.

In this book you'll discover key insights into Daniels character and his relevance for our generation. Aaron plainly articulates and supports the revelatory nature of Daniel and how this spirit will function in our day. Furthermore, the author also lays a blueprint to achieve that place in God to become people of insight, wisdom and revelation who influence every cultural arena including the arts, government, business, and everyday life.

This book also identifies various obstacles that we must eradicate in our lives and within the church in order to function in our promised destiny. Such noble attributes as unity, character, maturity, and power are all highlighted in these pages with practical ways to incorporate them into our lives by utilizing both biblical understanding and present day life experiences.

Although the content of this book is intended to prepare leadership it is also written in clear concise ways that can be understood by any sincere Christian seeking God's heart for this day. There is a resounding clarion call placed upon this generation to do the works that Jesus did and even greater works. As fantastic as that may sound, it will become a reality. Clearly, Aaron and Jill Marie Evans have been raised up to help bring this generation into that prophetic fulfillment.

For those with "eyes to see and ears to hear," a new spiritual corridor of divine possibility will be opened through the pages of this book. It is with a sense of honor and appreciation that I recommend this book to any desperate believer who desires to know the Lord fully and become a member of The Daniel Company.

Paul Keith Davis
WHITE DOVE MINISTRIES

ENDORSEMENTS

"Aaron has captured God's heart for this generation—the Emerging Daniel generation! Full of revelation and living understanding Aaron takes us through the pages of Daniel to bring fresh impartation for each one who 'eats' this scroll. God has blessed Aaron with what we need to hear. Be one of those 'watchers' and one of the 'wise' who will read, understand, and walk in the light shining from this book. Get ready for the seer gift to be more understood as you open its pages. This is the kind of book each leader and intercessor and teacher needs to read for the days to come!"

Dr. Brian Simmons
Apostolic Resource Center

"As long as we have known Aaron, he has been an amazing dispenser of wisdom and passion to see this generation rise up to become Daniels in both the church and the marketplace. This book is a much needed tool in helping us understand how to partner with God in discerning the times and seasons He is releasing upon the earth. This authoritative work made us ponder its truth, laugh, as well as yearn, for the coming of the

Daniels. By explaining and outlining steps that bring clarity to the practical side, we all are able to walk in the Daniel anointing and authority. What a revelation! We highly recommend this book!"

David & Josette Allen
Senior Pastors, Five Rivers Vineyard
Directors, Iformata Communications LLC

"Throughout the pages of this book, Aaron inspires and equips those who have a passion to be part of the emerging Daniel Company. This book guides us to understanding the Daniel qualities necessary to partner with the emerging Daniel Company. It offers inspiration in righteousness and wisdom for modeling your life after the characteristics of Daniel. Get ready for your understanding of the prophetic to become revolutionized as you read each informative and inspiring page!"

Sara E. Trollinger M.A.
Founder & President
National House of Hope

"In the more than 15 years that I have known Aaron Evans, I have observed the maturing of the call of God on his life. He has been an inspiring example to my family and many others of a man submitted to the discipline and training of the Lord through times of intimacy, personal study of His Word and His Nature, and dedicating the time required to listen to and learn to hear the Voice of the Lord. Likewise, he has submitted himself to that sometimes difficult process of serving other ministers and ministries of God, helping them to press through challenges in order to succeed in order to overcome. In so many ways, his life parallels that of Daniel. I believe he has been qualified by the Lord to assemble, prepare and lead this coming emerging Daniel Company to accomplish the works of the Lord in these coming days. If you are one of those emerging Daniels, read this book!"

D.M. Ken Johnson, Jr. DDS
Oral & Maxillofacial Surgery

"Aaron Evans' book, The Emerging Daniel Company, is like a road map of understanding to Christianity. Through his own profound experience he brings insight and perspective that will cause you to take your destiny and put it into action! This isn't just a prophetic perspective building book, it is an activator! The theme of the emerging Daniels is one of my favorites and I haven't heard anyone bring such practical depth to unload it like this. From the beginning to the defining of this generation in the end, after reading this book you will know how to place your feet in understanding for today."

Shawn Bolz, Senior Pastor
Expression58—Hollywood California
Author of *Keys to Heaven's Economy* and
The Throne Room Company

Are you part of the Emerging Daniel Company? The first requirement for pursuing a God-given strategy is to realize we need to have a strategy. If you think worship and economics are two unrelated topics that don't belong in the same book, your eyes are about to be opened. With a prophetic voice for the times we live in, Aaron Evans declares, "There is an overcoming company of people arising ... harvesters of the great harvest." With passion and clarity, Aaron proclaims vital truths we must apprehend if we are to "finish strong during this transitional season." I know Aaron and Jill-Marie, and they live a life of worship and service before our Lord. Your vision will be enlarged by this fresh strategy Aaron lays out in this book. I recommend this book and him.

Cal Beverly
Editor and publisher
The Citizen Newspapers
Fayetteville, Ga.

Table of Contents

CHAPTER ONE

DARE TO BE A DANIEL

Something amazing is happening in the spiritual realm right now. People and events are falling into place. Breakthroughs are occurring at an accelerated rate. Seals on long-hidden mysteries are being opened. God is developing an extraordinary generation for an extraordinary time! This is the Daniel Company, following the ancient prophet's example in righteousness and wisdom.

In 1988, the Lord told me that the only biblical book I was allowed to study was the Book of Daniel. I could read other Scripture, but I was supposed to meditate on Daniel. I needed to learn it, study it, and consume it. So I read it again and again and again.

After a few months, I began to feel my heart change. "I know this," I said to myself, slipping into boredom as I flipped open to Daniel Chapter 1 for what seemed like the millionth time.

"You don't know this!" the Lord thundered back. "You haven't even begun to touch the surface!"

So, I revived my energy and kept studying Daniel and again inquired of the Lord, "Why Daniel?" The Lord responded, "Daniel is a *prototype* of what is needed in the kingdom."

As I continued to study the book of Daniel, a number of things became illuminated and I began to understand why it was so important for me to become entrenched in this book. First, the book of Daniel is key to all biblical prophecy. Second, it challenged the faithful to stay alert (be watchful) and ready and to move accordingly. Third is that the political history of the times of the Gentiles is already recorded. Further, it shows that the Kingdom message boldly empowers the angelic to co-labor with us. And it shows that our God is the Living God who changes times and seasons and removes kings and raises up kings.

After years of what seemed like eating, living, and breathing the Book of Daniel, I made another important discovery. Daniel's mission was not to merely prophesy the end times and other important events; he was a biblical forerunner of an entire end-times generation. He was a model to the believers of our day, offering a vital example of purity and authority to a righteous generation anointed with revelatory insight. Like Daniel, we can probe deep into the heart of God and embrace His mysteries. We can enter into the promise Jesus made in John 8:12: *I am the light of the world. He who follows Me shall not walk in darkness, but have the light of life.*

I cannot overstate how important Daniel's example is to this generation. We must examine this prototype and contend to be filled with the knowledge of His will in all wisdom and spiritual understanding (Colossians 1:9). As an emerging company we must contend for the Spirit of Understanding, which includes understanding the times. We need to investigate Daniel's prophecy of a generation of shining stars, pointing the way to the Brilliant One. We need to rediscover the level of righteousness and purity God wants to bring us to. We must learn what unity, intimacy, and maturity can birth in our lives. In this season of human history, there must emerge a people who are wholly devoted to the Lord, who walk in love, true spiritual authority and power and for whom being filled with the fullness of God is their personal prayer and desire (Ephesians 3:19).

In Daniel 10, we gain insight into Daniel's character development. He had great intimacy with God, and heaven held this prophet in high esteem. When Daniel was visited by an angel, heaven's affection for him was evident: *O man greatly beloved* (Daniel 10:19). Daniel wasn't just loved in heaven—he was **greatly beloved.** Wouldn't it be incredible to be awakened from your bed and told by an angel that you were greatly beloved in heaven?

The moment I understood the magnitude of this statement, I knew I wanted to be like Daniel. I wanted the same spiritual vitamins he took and to learn everything he did. I wanted to know how his intercession moved angels to disrupt the demonic kingdom. I wanted to see the kingdom of heaven break through on earth. Those two words, *greatly beloved*, became a motivating force in my life.

Daniel was full of righteousness and wisdom. Even those who hated him knew he was wise and discerning. He and his three friends—Hananiah, Mishael and Azariah (whose names were changed by the king to Shedrach, Meshach and Abednego)—had a special relationship with God. It was this deep intimacy that opened incredible revelation to Daniel. In his lifetime, he spoke with angels and prophesied the theology and resurrection of the Messiah. Daniel foretold the rise of the antichrist, the Gentile empires, the second coming of Christ, and the end-time judgment of the world. In his lifetime, Daniel demonstrated the superiority of God over occult activities and earthly kingdoms.

MORE THAN A PROPHET

Daniel's example is important for anyone wanting to walk in divine wisdom. Ezekiel highlighted Daniel as a model of both wisdom and righteousness. Daniel was the standard by which other wise men and women were measured: *Behold, you are wiser than Daniel! There is no secret that can be hidden from you* (Ezekiel 28:3). Several chapters earlier, Ezekiel mentioned Daniel, along with Noah and Job, as measures of righteousness (Ezekiel 14:14). Here was a seer/prophet, profoundly gifted in his own right, highlighting the wisdom and righteousness of Daniel. Daniel was an example Ezekiel wanted to follow.

Generations later, the Apostle James expressed this idea of heavenly wisdom:

> *Who is wise and understanding among you? Let him show by good conduct that his works are done in the meekness of wisdom.*
>
> *But if you have bitter envy and self-seeking in your hearts, do not boast and lie against the truth.*
>
> *This wisdom does not descend from above, but is earthly, sensual, demonic.*
>
> *For where envy and self-seeking exist, confusion and every evil thing are there.*
>
> *But the wisdom that is from above is first pure, then peaceable, gentle, willing to yield, full of mercy and good fruits, without partiality and without hypocrisy.*
>
> *Now the fruit of righteousness is sown in peace by those who make peace* (James 3:13-18).

James outlined seven attributes of wisdom, and Daniel exemplified all of them. He:

Embraced purity
Loved peace
Was gentle, or, in some translations, "considerate"
Was willing to yield to another's righteousness
Was full of mercy and compassion
Was fair (just) to all, showing no partiality
Was without hypocrisy

The scriptures have much to say concerning righteousness and how those in Christ are called "the righteous." Proverbs 15:9 says the Lord loves those who follow righteousness. Isaiah 32:1 states: *Behold a king will reign in righteousness. The righteous will come through trouble.* Proverbs 12:13 says that the "righteous will be recompensed." "When things go well for the righteous the city rejoices" and that "the righteous are as bold as a lion." "The Lord is our righteousness."

God is restoring the pattern of wisdom and righteousness demonstrated by Daniel to those who will follow it today.

GOD GIVES WISDOM

Wisdom in the Greek is *sophia,* which is insight into the true nature of things. In Proverbs 4 and 8, wisdom is referred to as a *person* and the *principle thing to have.*

Daniel 2:20 reveals that wisdom and might belong to Him. It was by wisdom the Lord founded the Earth. We are instructed to get wisdom and understanding. Psalm 90:12 says, *"So teach us to number our days that we may gain a heart of wisdom."*

In Proverbs 2:1-17, we are shown how we can enhance Godly wisdom. We are to receive it and treasure it. We are to incline our ears and apply our hearts, crying out and lifting up our voices. Wisdom is to be sought after. Wisdom and understanding in Proverbs 8:1 is both personified by being a "she": *"She, Wisdom takes her stand by the gates and entry of the cities. She warns the simple to desire an understanding heart. Wisdom dwells with prudence and finds out witty invention* (8:12).

In Hebrews 13:7-8, we are instructed to follow the example of the righteous people who have walked before us: *Remember those who rule over you, who have spoken the word of God to you, whose faith follow, considering the outcome of their conduct. Jesus Christ is the same yesterday, today, and forever.*

We must weigh any spiritual model by the words of Hebrews 13:7-8. If we will study their faith, their lifestyle, and how they encountered God, we need to ask, "What did they do to attract God to themselves?" Then we will discover how we can draw God to ourselves.

I want to know what I have to do to attract God to me. I don't ever want to be without Him, not even for a moment. We should not settle for where we are at currently. We should strive for a deeper, fuller, and greater relationship with God. Every day should be better than the last. I want to experience a higher revelation of kingdom principles—don't you? Daniel hung out with angels and learned the mysteries of the Messiah and the end times. Who wouldn't want that?

Hebrews 6:11-12 states *"And we desire that each one of you show the same diligence to the full assurance of hope until the end, that you do not become sluggish, but imitate those who through faith and patience inherit the promises.* It takes faith and patience to walk the same path as those who were called "righteous"; we have to be diligent and persevere. God never promised it would be easy, but He did say it would come to pass if we remained *faithful* to His call.

PREPARATION BEFORE PROMOTION

What was the secret to Daniel's success and greatness? In looking at the prayer life of Daniel illustrated in 6:10, we see it was his private prayer life that empowered his heart to be strong and confident. His kneeling in prayer was his recognition of the supremacy and greatness of his God. When Daniel read Jeremiah 33:3 he knew that he was instructed to call unto Him and that He would not only answer, but show great and mighty things! I like the amplified version, which says in verse 3: *Call to me and I will answer you and show you great and mighty things; fenced in and hidden, which you do not know, do not distinguish and recognize, have knowledge of and understand.*

We should note that Daniel's model of prayer provides breakthrough to things "fenced in." Developing specific times to pray (something to say for consistency) and finding a place or places where you meet with Him allow God to connect with us heart to heart so that His plans and His purposes for our lives and those for whom we have responsibility can be revealed. Spending time in this way teaches us to wait, watch and listen. It causes us to grow in sensitivity to His Spirit, offering us the ability to recognize what the Spirit is doing in the lives of others.

Fasting, especially what is commonly referred to as the "Daniel fast" also increases our ability to move in revelation and demonstration of the realities of heaven that need to manifest on Earth. What is the "Daniel fast"? It is a partial fast in which *some* foods are restricted. It is a biblical-based fast that is modeled after the experiences of Daniel mentioned in Chapter 1 and Chapter 10.

In Chapter 1, Daniel requested that they (he and his friends, Hananiah, Mishael and Azariah) be given a test. Some versions say they ate only vegetables; others say "pulse" to eat and water to drink. (Pulse was food that originated from seed). A Daniel fast has no set time. I personally like the ten days in which they were rewarded by God with "supernatural learning" (1:17). God gave them knowledge and skill in all literature and wisdom. The "learning" was actually the ability to discern the false from the true as they resided among the Babylonian culture. This wisdom included diplomacy and "statecraft." A great book detailing the Daniel fast is written by Susan Gregory.

The process of being separated unto His purposes is a requirement for all who are called by Him. The purpose of separation is non-conformity to the world and its ways. Having a life that is cleansed from defilement while demonstrating faithfulness and purity in the face of adversity is the essence of being separated (Hebrews 2:11).

IMPEDING OUR INHERITANCE

The scripture names certain practices that hinder us from inheriting the Kingdom and walking in the fullness of our destiny. We are instructed to have our bloodline cleansed from the sins of our fathers (Exodus 20:5), and to reprove the works of darkness is a command (Ephesians 5:10-12).

We can find nine *forbidden* practices of the occult listed in Deuteronomy 18:10-11 occurring among the people, and Acts 19:18-20 depicts the result of the occult exposed. We can recognize several of these portrayed in our present-day entertainment as seemingly harmless:

1. Human sacrifice
2. Divination
3. Observer of times (Astrology—which is more specifically, The study of the movements and relative positions of celestial bodies and their supposed influence on human affairs
4. Enchanter—one who uses seductive spells
5. Witchcraft
6. Charmer—possessing the ability to manipulate objects
7. Consulter with familiar spirits
8. Wizard—practitioner of magical arts
9. Necromancer—one who contacts the dead

Also in 1John 2:15-16, we are admonished to *"not love the world system for all that is in it is the lust of the flesh, the lust of the eyes and the pride of life."* In our present culture, pride, which God hates, is a major issue (Proverbs 6:16-19). God resists the proud and

Proverbs tells us that "pride goes before destruction" and a "haughty spirit before a fall." It was pride that caused the fall of Lucifer (Isaiah 14:12-14). In Daniel Chapter 4, God took a king and brought him to humility. As we learn to humble ourselves under the mighty hand of God, He will exalt us in due time. Honoring the Lord and being loyal to Him will prove us worthy of promotion in the ways of the kingdom.

> *The eyes of the Lord run to and fro throughout the whole earth to show Himself strong on behalf of those whose heart is loyal to him.* (2Chronicles 16:9).

Daniel and his companions proved their loyalty and thus were rewarded by God. In Daniel 1:17, it says that God gave them knowledge (knowledge had to do with reasoning skills and thought processes) and skill in all literature (science and arts) and wisdom (diplomacy and statecraft). They were given the ability to discern the nature of things and to interpret them in their true light.

Supernatural learning is available to those who will present themselves to the Lord, prepare their hearts to be free from the fear of men, self-promotion, ambition and being "man-pleasers." Studying to show ourselves approved unto God and being a student of the Word, having a Biblical worldview is also required. Perseverance, humility, and obedience bring promotion from the only One truly empowered to promote. Psalm 75:6-7 says, "*Promotion comes not from the east nor from the west nor from the south, but God is the Judge. He puts down one and exalts another.*"

PROPHETIC DREAMS AND VISIONS
The Lord gives a prophetic dream to a wicked king revealing an outline of the history of the world in detail from the time of Nebuchadnezzar until the second

coming of Christ. This dream would later be termed the times of the Gentiles. This displays the foreknowledge of God concerning the rise and fall of empires and nations in advance.

Dreams and visions are some of the ways the God of heaven can and will speak to all and any—including kings, queens, presidents, senators, and congressmen, all of whom have one thing in common—they eventually need to sleep! If He cannot get you to listen in the day, He will get you to listen at night! The outpouring of the Spirit will release dreams and visions (Joel 2:28-29; Acts 2:17-21).

Early in Nebuchadnezzar's reign, the Babylonian king had a dream so troubling that he could not go back to sleep. The king gathered his wise men to get some answers. The biblical account is unclear as to whether Nebuchadnezzar could fully remember the dream or not; either way, he demanded that his advisors reveal to him what he had dreamed and then interpret it. The king wasn't going to make things easy on these wise men!

The Chaldeans were considered the highest priestly caste of the ancient world. The title carried weight as one who possessed superior occult powers and knowledge. When the Chaldean mystics were unable to give King Nebuchadnezzar the answer he sought, he ordered the death of all the wise men in Babylon, including Daniel and his friends, who had been renamed Shadrach, Meshach, and Abednego.

Daniel responded with counsel and wisdom by going to the king and requesting time to inquire of the God of heaven. Daniel, being a team player, called on his companions to come to his house where the atmosphere was rich with the presence of the Lord, to inquire and seek for mercies from the Most High God. Then, in a night vision, the secret was revealed to Daniel.

Blessed be the name of God forever and ever, for wisdom and might are His. He changes the times and the seasons. He removes kings and raises up kings. He gives wisdom to the wise and knowledge to those who have understanding. He reveals deep and secret things. He knows what is in the darkness and light dwells with Him. — Daniel 2:20-22

Daniel got an answer to his prayer almost immediately. Wouldn't you like to pray and be answered by God that quickly? Boldly, Daniel went to the king, revealed the details of the dream, and interpreted (*to explain difficult information or thoughts in terms that the hearer can easily understand*) its meaning.

The dream was about an image whose head was of fine gold, its chest and arms of silver, its belly and thighs of bronze, its legs of iron and its feet of partly iron and partly clay. (History has revealed that these represented five different empires in which four have risen and fallen and that we are currently witnessing the implementation of the fifth through the formation of the European Common Market.) Then there was a stone cut without hands that destroyed the image and became a great mountain that fills the whole earth (Daniel 2:34-35), symbolic of the Kingdom of God being established in all the earth.

Throughout the meeting with Nebuchadnezzar, Daniel gave glory to God for the revelation. He was so steadfast in his assertion that God was the source for unlocking the mystery that the king himself declared in Daniel 2:47, *Truly, your God is the God of gods, the Lord of kings, and a revealer of secrets, since you could reveal this secret.*

PARALLELS TO DANIEL

The similarities between Daniel's ancient time and the current era are many. For one, Daniel was called to a righteous life in the midst of a corrupt culture. The tests facing Daniel and his three friends started as soon as they arrived in Babylon. The king's steward offered them all manner of food and drink, but the young Hebrews refused anything but vegetables and water, because they did not want to be defiled in God's sight.

This captured God's attention. It drew a line in the sand between the four men and the rest of the leaders in Nebuchadnezzar's kingdom. Daniel 1:17 speaks of that spiritual favor: *As for these four young men, God gave them knowledge and skill in all literature and wisdom; and Daniel had understanding in all visions and dreams.* God's favor transformed them to where even the king noted something different about the four.

> *Then the king interviewed them, and among them all none was found like Daniel, Hananiah, Mishael, and Azariah; therefore they served before the king.*
>
> *And in all matters of wisdom and understanding about which the king examined them, he found them ten times better than all the magicians and astrologers who were in all his realm* (Daniel 1:19-20).

From the moment he arrived in pagan Babylon, Daniel grew continuously in his ability to understand spiritual realities and the ways of the Lord. That ability blossomed when Daniel revealed and provided understanding of the king's dreams. We read that Daniel remained calm and confident when difficult times arose. His primary mission was always clear—he wanted to glorify God. He never took credit for himself; instead he pointed the attention of the most powerful men in the world to the One True God. All of this was done through just one man. Can you imagine what could be accomplished by an entire generation of people like him?

In Daniel 3, Shadrach, Meshach, and Abednego faced their own test. Would they bow before Nebuchadnezzar's golden idol or face the fiery furnace? It is one of the most noted stories recorded in Scripture. The young men refused Nebuchadnezzar's order, and were thrown into a furnace so hot that the guards who carried them in died instantly. However, the three Hebrews stood in the midst of the fire unscathed, meeting the Son of God face-to-face.

Daniel faced a similar test with the new king, a Mede named Darius, as he rose in reputation. Daniel's political opponents wanted to crush him, but they didn't have much to work with.

> So the governors and satraps sought to find some charge against Daniel concerning the kingdom; but they could find no charge or fault, because he was faithful; nor was there any error or fault found in him.
> Then these men said, "We shall not find any charge against this Daniel unless we find it against him concerning the law of his God" (Daniel 6:4-5).

In other words, Daniel was refined and faithful. Even when the other officials conspired against him and forced Darius's hand, the godless king knew Daniel would survive. Moments before Daniel was put into a den of lions, Darius said: *Your God, whom you serve continually, He will deliver you* (Daniel 6:16).

The accuracy of Darius's prophetic word was never in doubt. We see that Daniel's integrity and humility in the face of certain death inspired Darius:

Now the king went to his palace and spent the night fasting; and no musicians were brought before him. Also his sleep went from him.

Then the king arose very early in the morning and went in haste to the den of lions.

And when he came to the den, he cried out with a lamenting voice to Daniel. The king spoke, saying to Daniel, "Daniel, servant of the living God, has your God, whom you serve continually, been able to deliver you from the lions?"

Then Daniel said to the king, "O king, live forever!

My God sent His angel and shut the lion's mouths, so that they have not hurt me, because I was found innocent before Him; and also, O king, I have done no wrong before you.

Now the king was exceedingly glad for him, and commanded that they should take Daniel up out of the den. So Daniel was taken up out of the den, and no injury whatever was found on him, because he believed in his God (Daniel 6:18-23).

The miracle so astounded Darius that the king sent out a new decree:

I make a decree that in every dominion of my kingdom men must tremble and fear before the God of Daniel. For He is the living God, and stead-fast forever; His kingdom is the one which shall not be destroyed, and His dominion shall endure to the end.

He delivers and rescues, and He works signs and wonders in heaven and on earth, who has delivered Daniel from the power of the lions (Daniel 6:26-27).

Again and again, Daniel proved himself worthy of God's favor. When a person walks in the favor of God, nothing will be impossible for him or her; which is very evident in Daniel's life. His ability to see the future increased even as his faith was strengthened.

HOUSE OF THE WATCHFUL – HOUSE OF THE WISE

As I continued my study of Daniel, I was gripped by the prophet's passion for God and his integrity in life. Then on my fiftieth birthday, my spiritual father, friend and mentor, Bob Jones (an international prophetic seer), had a vision that pushed me forward in my understanding of the Daniel example.

In his vision, Bob and I were out walking together. As we walked, he showed me what he called the House of the Watchful and the House of the Wise. At that time the land was desolate, and those who had previously occupied it had been found wanting by God and were pulled from it. Some had tried to sell it for fame, an act God despised. Their time was up and the land was ready for new occupants. Unfortunately, the unrighteous had inherited it; the enemy had stolen the territory. However, God had a plan to restore this stolen land seven times over. In short order, the evil tenants were burned out. Bob knew the house was his to give away, and he knew that he wanted to give it to me, a spiritual son. So he did, and the house became my house. It was a spiritual bloodline gift and inheritance. As he left the vision, Bob was reminded of Isaiah 49:8:

> In an acceptable time I have heard You, and in the day of salvation I have helped You; I will preserve You and give You as a covenant to the people, to restore the earth, to cause them to inherit the desolate heritages.

In further conversations with Bob, and through my reflection on the Book of Daniel, I learned more about these two houses. Watchers, so named because they are on watch (in the spiritual realm) for the Lord, are intercessors who find it difficult to stick with a human agenda of things to pray. These watchers rest before the Lord and pray for what He reveals to them. Bob calls these intercessors "wild geese," which paints a perfect picture of their call. In the natural, no one can sneak up on a wild goose without it letting everyone within earshot know about it. Geese naturally fly in a formation that supports one another, in unison and in rank. In the same way, watchers are sensitive to the wiles, schemes and strategies of the Evil One. They function in agreement and in protocol. These watchers are responsible for transmitting information about God's presence and enemy activity to the House of the Wise.

The House of the Wise are the mature apostolic and prophetic voices. They have a good biblical grounding in scripture and are growing in comprehensive insight into His ways and purposes with the anointing to solve problems. They are especially empowered with the Spirit of Wisdom, Understanding, Counsel and Might. It was said of Daniel by the queen in Chapter Five (10-12) that Daniel had: (1) the Spirit of the Holy God, (2) an excellent spirit, (3) knowledge, (4) understanding, (5) interpretation of dreams, (6) solving "riddles," (7) solving problems and explaining enigmas. These are what I would call the "Seven-Fold" anointing.

Together, the watchful and the wise contend for supernatural insight and application for our families, churches, cities, states, and regions. They live in freshness, friendship, and favor, just as Daniel did. They walk in the ways of the Lord, as laid out in Colossians 1:9-12 [Amplified]:

> *For this reason we also, from the day we heard of it, have not ceased to pray and make [special] request for you, [asking] that you may be filled with the full [deep and clear] knowledge of His will*

in all spiritual wisdom, [in comprehensive insight into the ways and purposes of God] and in understanding and discernment of spiritual things—

That you may walk [live and conduct yourselves] in a manner worthy of the Lord, fully pleasing to Him and desiring to please Him in all things, bearing fruit in every good work and steadily growing and increasing in and by the knowledge of God [with fuller, deeper, and clearer insight, acquaintance, and recognition].

[We pray] that you may be invigorated and strengthened with all power according to the might of His glory, [to exercise] every kind of endurance and patience [perseverance and forbearance] with joy,

Giving thanks to the Father, Who has qualified and made us fit to share the portion which is the inheritance of the saints [God's holy people] in the Light.

It is up to the wise to look at the revelation and information coming in from the watchers whose anointing is to see things in the Spirit, and see what the enemy is up to. Those who are ordained by the Lord are graced to interpret it with spiritual understanding. Together, they are to join the pieces to see and understand what the Spirit is saying. If there ever was a time we need to know what the Spirit is saying, it is now. One of the things being said is that we need to reclaim and restore spiritual and natural inheritances that were once occupied by the righteous, but now are in the hands of the enemy who have made them desolate. We must rebuild the old ruins, raise up former desolations, and repair ruined cities for the glory of God.

The Spirit of the Lord GOD is upon Me, because the LORD has anointed Me to preach good tidings to the poor; He has sent Me to heal the broken-hearted, to proclaim liberty to the captives, and the opening of the prison to those who are bound;

to proclaim the acceptable year of the LORD, and the day of vengeance of our God; to comfort all who mourn,

to console those who mourn in Zion, to give them beauty for ashes, the oil of joy for mourning, the garment of praise for the spirit of heaviness; that they may be called trees of righteousness, the planting of the LORD, that He may be glorified.

And they shall rebuild the old ruins, they shall raise up the former desolations, and they shall repair the ruined cities, the desolations of many generations.

Strangers shall stand and feed your flocks, and the sons of the foreigner shall be your plowmen and your vinedressers.

But you shall be named the priests of the LORD, they shall call you the servants of our God. You shall eat the riches of the Gentiles, and in their glory you shall boast.

Instead of your shame you shall have double honor, and instead of confusion they shall rejoice in their portion. Therefore in their land they shall possess double; everlasting joy shall be theirs.

For I, the LORD, love justice; I hate robbery for burnt offering; I will direct their work in truth, and will make with them an everlasting covenant.

Their descendants shall be known among the Gentiles, and their offspring among the people. All who see them shall acknowledge them, that they are the posterity whom the LORD has blessed.

I will greatly rejoice in the LORD, my soul shall be joyful in my God; for He has clothed me with the garments of salvation, He has covered me with the robe of righteousness, as a bridegroom decks

*himself with ornaments, and as a bride adorns
herself with her jewels.*

*For as the earth brings forth its bud, as the
garden causes the things that are sown in it to
spring forth, so the Lord GOD will cause righteousness and praise to spring forth before all the
nations* (Isaiah 61:1-11)

What is the key to opening the doors of these houses
for the watchers, prophetic intercessors and the wise? It
is a character trait we see time and again in Daniel's life:
Humility. The presence and power of the Glorified One
come to those that have humble spirits.(Luke 18:14).
Humbling ourselves does not mean self-degradation or
false modesty; rather it is a life that depends on the life
of the Lord flowing through them. Isaiah 57:15 says,
*The High and Lofty One dwells in high and holy places
with those of contrite and humble spirit.* By his example,
Daniel's life teaches us that humility is about directing
the glory for our successes to God—not receiving the
praises of men for ourselves.

THE LIFE OF DANIEL—A BLUEPRINT FOR
END-TIME FORERUNNERS

Daniel was a forerunner in his generation, but he
also serves as a prototype for an end of the age "forerunner company" that the Lord is commissioning to prepare the nations to receive Christ at His second coming.
While some believers continue to remain heroes only
in their daydreams and vain imaginations, Daniel, the
Hebrew prophet in exile, gives us a portrait of a real,
weak human being who, when confronted with difficult
options, time and time again purposed in his heart to
give himself to the Lord in secret (Daniel 1:8) as well
as before the eyes of men (Daniel 6:10). Because of
this he was rewarded with divine revelation, not just
for his generation (to pray for the end of Babylonian

exile and prepare Israel for continuing discipline and ultimate deliverance), but he was also given some of the most detailed eschatological revelation relevant for this generation.

In many ways, there should be some sense of gratitude that Daniel did not waver in his devotion to the Lord. His obedience and loyalty give us a blueprint to study and help prepare us for what is coming. He has given us a roadmap of the tenor of men and women we must be to not only confront the greatest foe of Christ and His bride to ever walk on the earth (Daniel 11:32-36), but also to escort us in the greatest outpouring of the Holy Spirit the earth has yet to witness.

Daniel is not to be viewed as a historical anomaly, rather as a prototype of the forerunner that the Lord is raising up at the end of the age who will confront darkness, bind kings with chains, nobles with fetters of iron, and execute the written judgment of God (Psalm 149:8-9). His life of faithfulness should be viewed as an invitation to everyone and anyone who is willing to become an overcomer and respond to the Lord's call.

The Book of Daniel was not written in chronological order. The twelve chapters give us understanding of progressive revelation to prepare us for the times of the end. Here is Daniel in its chronological order:

Chapter One—Babylonian captivity
Chapter Two—Nebuchadnezzar's dream
Chapter Three—Nebuchadnezzar's image
Chapter Four—Nebuchadnezzar's pride
Chapter Seven—**The** time of the Gentiles
Chapter Eight—Ram and He-goat vision
Chapter Five—Babylon falls to Persians
Chapter Nine—Vision of seventy weeks
Chapter Six—The lion's den
Chapters Ten through Twelve—Times of the end.

There are five prophetic phases that are repeated throughout the Book of Daniel and this book to help you experience and live a victorious life, and navigate the perilous times we are in. They are: (1).separation, (2) revelation, (3) promotion, (4) domination, (kingdom advancement), (5) transition.

PROPHETIC INTERCESSION

Prophetic intercession is the ability to receive prayer requests from the Lord and pray them with the utterance being anointed to fulfill its purpose. Daniel modeled Spirit-empowered praying throughout the Book of Daniel. I like James Goll's definition of prophetic intercession. He said that it is waiting before God in order to hear or receive God's burden (which means God's concern, warning conditions, vision, promise or word), and then responding back to the Lord and to the people with appropriate actions (Jim Goll's book, *Prayer Storm*, page 70).

With prophetic intercession, the priestly and prophetic are functioning together. Intercessors become prophetic when flowing in this spirit current. Often they will be led to plead promises given by the Lord as Daniel did. He picked up the baton that was given to the previous generation and presented it to the Lord.

> *In the first year of his reign I, Daniel, understood by the books the number of the years specified by the word of the Lord through Jeremiah the prophet that He would accomplish seventy years in the desolations of Jerusalem.*
>
> *Then I set my face toward the Lord God to make request by prayer and supplications, with fasting, sackcloth, and ashes.*
>
> *And I prayed to the Lord my God, and made confession, and said, "O Lord, great and awesome God, who keeps His covenant and mercy with*

those who love Him, and with those who keep His commandments,

we have sinned and committed iniquity, we have done wickedly and rebelled, even by departing from Your precepts and Your judgments.

Neither have we heeded Your servants the prophets, who spoke in Your name to our kings and our princes, to our fathers and all the people of the land.

O Lord, righteousness belongs to You, but to us shame of face, as it is this day—to the men of Judah, to the inhabitants of Jerusalem and all Israel, those near and those far off in all the countries to which You have driven them, because of the unfaithfulness which they have committed against You.

"O Lord, to us belongs shame of face, to our kings, our princes, and our fathers, because we have sinned against You.

To the Lord our God belong mercy and forgiveness, though we have rebelled against Him.

We have not obeyed the voice of the Lord our God, to walk in His laws, which He set before us by His servants the prophets.

Yes, all Israel has transgressed Your law, and has departed so as not to obey Your voice; therefore the curse and the oath written in the Law of Moses the servant of God have been poured out on us, because we have sinned against Him.

And He has confirmed His words, which He spoke against us and against our judges who judged us, by bringing upon us a great disaster; for under the whole heaven such has never been done as what has been done to Jerusalem.

"As it is written in the Law of Moses, all this disaster has come upon us; yet we have not made

our prayer before the Lord our God, that we might turn from our iniquities and understand Your truth.

Therefore the Lord has kept the disaster in mind, and brought it upon us; for the Lord our God is righteous in all the works which He does, though we have not obeyed His voice.

And now, O Lord our God, who brought Your people out of the land of Egypt with a mighty hand, and made Yourself a name, as it is this day—we have sinned, we have done wickedly!

"O Lord, according to all Your righteousness, I pray, let Your anger and Your fury be turned away from Your city Jerusalem, Your holy mountain; because for our sins, and for the iniquities of our fathers, Jerusalem and Your people are a reproach to all those around us.

Now therefore, our God, hear the prayer of Your servant, and his supplications, and for the Lord's sake cause Your face to shine on Your sanctuary, which is desolate.

O my God, incline Your ear and hear; open Your eyes and see our desolations, and the city which is called by Your name; for we do not present our supplications before You because of our righteous deeds, but because of Your great mercies.

O Lord, hear! O Lord, forgive! O Lord, listen and act! Do not delay for Your own sake, my God, for Your city and Your people are called by Your name" (Daniel 9:2-19).

Daniel was a seer whose life demonstrated the power of a fervent, effective prayer life. It had incredible impact in the heavens and the unseen realms. He received insight with understanding concerning the seventy weeks prophecy that pertains to the unveiling of the revelation of the Messiah and the antichrist (Daniel

9:22-27) and also what the scriptures call "the times of the end" (Daniel 12:9).

Intercessors and watchers must be worshippers devoted to seeking Him and knowing what He wants to do. True worshippers carry four requirements. The first is a true heart; second is fullness of faith; third is a heart sprinkled from an evil conscience; and fourth is our bodies washed with pure water (Hebrews 10:22). Prophetic intercessors are worshippers who develop intimacy with Him.

Prophetic intercession is discerning the wisdom of God concerning a person, place or situation. It is praying in agreement with His leading and direction. His spiritual wisdom usually comes through revelatory gifts (the Word of Knowledge, Word of Wisdom, Prophecy and Discerning of Spirits). It is activated by prophetic promises and also waiting upon the Lord to discern what is on His heart. Prophetic intercession is released by prayer, declarations, proclamations and decrees in order to advance kingdom purposes.

CHAPTER TWO

THE SHINING ONES: PURITY

Daniel's example of purity and wisdom is especially necessary today. We are contending to be a righteous generation, anointed with the spirit of revelation and insight. When we step out in unity, intimacy, and maturity, we shine brightly in a dark world. We guide people to the Source of all light: Jesus Christ.

God gave Daniel a prophetic word about the end times. It is this verse that defines the Emerging Daniel Company:

> *Those who are wise shall shine like the brightness of the firmament, and those who turn many to righteousness like the stars forever and ever* (Daniel 12:3).

The way to shine brightly is simple: We need to love Him with all of our hearts, minds, souls, and strength. When we return to that first love, He moves heaven and earth to meet us. We can access the wisdom of God to direct our own journeys when we throw out the unbelief and doubt that plagues most of us. It is as easy as declaring to God our desire to fulfill the call on our lives. "I will be anointed with the Spirit of revelation," we can pray. "I will walk with You in Your ways and wisdom. I will not live in unbelief."

As Believers, we all need to grow in spiritual virtue that will make us strong enough to handle the presence and plan of God with both skill and understanding. No true follower of God wants to settle for mediocrity; we want to be the best vessel we can be. By striving to be a "shining one" who will turn many to righteousness, we purify ourselves and impart purity to others. John the Baptist did just this. In John 5:35, Jesus explained the importance of His cousin's witness—*"He was the burning and shining lamp, and you were willing for a time to rejoice in his light."* But John, like Daniel, never took the glory for himself. Instead, he used his light to focus people's attention on Jesus Christ Himself, as we read in John 3:27–36:

> *John answered and said, "A man can receive nothing unless it has been given to him from heaven.*
>
> *"You yourselves bear me witness that I said, 'I am not the Christ,' but, 'I have been sent before Him.'*
>
> *"He who has the bride is the bridegroom; but the friend of the bridegroom, who stands and hears him, rejoices greatly because of the bridegroom's voice. Therefore this joy of mine is fulfilled.*
>
> *"He must increase, but I must decrease.*
>
> *He who comes from above is above all; he who is of the earth is earthly and speaks of the earth. He who comes from heaven is above all.*
>
> *"And what He has seen and heard, that He testifies; and no one receives His testimony.*
>
> *"He who has received His testimony has certified that God is true.*
>
> *"For He whom God has sent speaks the words of God, for God does not give the Spirit by measure.*

"The Father loves the Son, and has given all things into His hand.

"He who believes in the Son has everlasting life; and he who does not believe the Son shall not see life, but the wrath of God abides on him."

John's spirit reflected the brightness of the Lord, but he knew he did not own that honor. Instead, it came from the light of God, and everything he said and did was meant to focus more attention on the Lord. Like Daniel and John, we need to have ears tuned to hear God. We need to ask for fresh anointing every day, never relying on yesterday's ideas or revelation to sustain us, but always asking God for more of His presence. We need His quickening Spirit to be within us.

THE PURIFICATION PROCESS

In Daniel 12:10, we read what separates the Emerging Daniel Company from those around them: *"Many shall be purified, made white, and refined, but the wicked shall do wickedly; and none of the wicked shall understand, but the wise shall understand."* These three declarations—purified, made white and refined—are vital qualities to fulfilling the call on our lives. Purity is an incredible gift from God. When we are cleansed by the blood of Christ, we are fully released from the contamination of sin. In short, the darkness in us is replaced by the light of Christ. When we are made white, we are without blemish and able to reflect all visible light. Imagine being an untainted reflection of the Father!

Refinement is the process by which purification is achieved. In Zechariah 13:9, we read more of what it means to be spiritually refined:

I will refine them as silver is refined, and test them as gold is tested. They will call on My name, and I will answer them. I will say, "This is

*My people"; and each one will say, "The LORD is
my God."*

Refinement removes any and all contamination that
would make us weaker, duller, or darker. It removes
both the impurity of sin and the damage it causes. The
Refiner's fire, about which we so often sing, heats our
spirit to a point where all of our character flaws surface and can be removed. The higher the heat and the
longer the application, the less impurity can remain.
The greater the purity and the brighter the light, the
clearer we are able to reflect Christ.

ACCELERATION

This process of refinement is happening faster than
ever before. I believe there has been a shift in the Spirit,
and that the prophecy of Haggai 2:6–9 is now coming
to pass:

> *"For thus says the Lord of Hosts: 'Once more (it
> is a little while) I will shake heaven and earth, the
> sea and dry land;*
> *And I will shake all nations, and they shall
> come to the Desire of All Nations, and I will fill this
> temple with glory,' says the Lord of Hosts.*
> *'The silver is Mine, and the gold is Mine,' says
> the Lord of Hosts.*
> *'The glory of this latter temple shall be greater
> than the former,' says the LORD of Hosts. 'And in
> this place I will give peace,' says the LORD of Hosts."*

In Psalm 46:1–7, we read confirmation of this word that
God is shaking the earth:

> *God is our refuge and strength, a very present
> help in trouble.*

> *Therefore we will not fear, even though the earth be removed, and though the mountains be carried into the midst of the sea;*
>
> *Though its waters roar and be troubled, though the mountains shake with its swelling. Selah*
>
> *There is a river whose streams shall make glad the city of God, the holy place of the tabernacle of the Most High.*
>
> *God is in the midst of her, she shall not be moved; God shall help her, just at the break of dawn.*
>
> *The nations raged, the kingdoms were moved; He uttered His voice, the earth melted.*
>
> *The LORD of Hosts is with us; the God of Jacob is our refuge.*

Even with God shaking the nations, those who believe in Him will be safe. The promise of a river that *"shall make glad the city of God"* is a gift to each of us. If we stay in the flow of what His Holy Spirit is doing, we will have peace. Everything that can be shaken will be shaken by God. The heavens are shifting and the earth is following suit, but those who give themselves to the refining heat of God will be glad in Him.

Refinement hurts, no matter how fast it occurs. Heat is not a comfortable element for human beings. However, we must step out of the "yester-me, yester-you, yesterday" trap that ensnares so many Christians. We have to live in the now. God doesn't need more wounded, hurt, religious people; He needs humble vessels willing to reflect His glory.

The early church did not have this problem. They were so full of the Spirit and so in tune with His light that they would correctly and fully interpret prophecy. In Acts 2, the Apostle Peter, a simple, uneducated fisherman, took years of scriptural prophecy and interpreted them in light of his relationship with Jesus

Christ. Thousands were saved that day. John, Philip, James, and Paul all did the same.

I desperately want to see the House of the Wise take its place and interpret what the watchers have seen and sensed. More wisdom is the desire of my heart. It seems that since I first acknowledged Jesus Christ as my Lord and Savior, I have been given prophetic words about the gift of wisdom in my life. When I look around the church, I see a lot of revelation but very little insight and understanding. My desire is to teach people how to access the wisdom of God in every circumstance.

Some time ago, the Lord spoke to me about the next generation of believers. "You will walk in power and demonstration, but most of all you will be a part of My government that knows how to facilitate the movement but not control of My Spirit. Know that many of the wars you will go through are for your children and your children's children. Consider David, who had the vision and desire, but was not the one to build — it was Solomon who built and was able to live in peace. I will give you the desire and the vision, but I won't let you build it."

It takes real humility to be able to lay down your own dreams and instead pursue what God is forming. Many Christians who are suffering or struggling at the moment need to know that they are likely blazing a trail for the next generation. Many battles are fought for the sake of our children. My son, Josiah, will prove to have his start years ahead of me in his walk with God. Things I have contended for over the years will flow to him naturally, because he has grown up with it. It is a non-negotiable truth for him.

The Refiner's fire is a difficult furnace to live in, but the further ahead we can launch our children, the better. For forty years, Caleb and Joshua wandered in the desert with the Israelites, waiting for their generation to die so they could take the Promised Land. What a testimony those two had! In Joshua 14:7–11, we read how God's refining fire strengthened Caleb:

> *I was forty years old when Moses the servant of the LORD sent me from Kadesh Barnea to spy out the land, and I brought back word to him as it was in my heart.*
>
> *Nevertheless my brethren who went up with me made the heart of the people melt, but I wholly followed the LORD my God.*
>
> *So Moses swore on that day, saying, "Surely the land where your foot has trodden shall be your inheritance and your children's forever, because you have wholly followed the LORD my God."*
>
> *And now, behold, the LORD has kept me alive, as He said, these forty-five years, ever since the LORD spoke this word to Moses while I s r a e l wandered in the wilderness; and now, here I am this day, eighty-five years old.*
>
> *As yet I am as strong this day as on the day that Moses sent me; just as my strength was then, so now is my strength for war, both for going out and for coming in.*

While we are making a way for the next generation, we still receive the blessings of God for our own obedience and dedication to purity. When we believe God for His strength to persevere, we are given supernatural strength to endure.

Mature believers know that walking in the Spirit isn't just about the incredible highs of God. It is a journey through some pretty dismal lows, where the enemy attacks from every angle. Jesus' life is a perfect example: He went from the high of the Transfiguration to the low of every religious and political leader in the country wanting Him dead. The moment Jesus' destiny was spoken; all hell broke loose to stop Him. Those called to walk in the Daniel Company understand this dynamic and seek God's refinement and guidance every step of the way.

ACCESSING OUR DESTINY

Any of us can access the book of destiny that God has written about us. It isn't just for the "superstars" of our faith; it is for every believer who loves Him with all their heart. This emerging generation, through the prophecies in Daniel Chapter 12, has the incredible privilege of living in a destiny that will witness the unveiling of great mysteries and hidden secrets reserved for the "Times of the End." Mysteries are truths in Him that can only be revealed by Him, as we read in Colossians 2:2–3:

> *that their hearts may be encouraged, being knit together in love, and attaining to all riches of the full assurance of understanding, to the knowledge of the mystery of God, both of the Father and of Christ in whom are hidden all the treasures of wisdom and knowledge.*

God has kept things hidden *for* us, not *from* us. That's an important distinction, as He has been waiting for a company of people to grow in unity, intimacy, and maturity so He can trust them with these mysteries. God is looking for good stewards and a generation of faithfulness.

Accessing our destinies requires us to understand and use the spiritual law of declaration. In Hebrews 1:1–4, we read how Jesus obtained His name:

> *God, who at various times and in various ways spoke in times past to the fathers by the prophets, has in these last days spoken to us by His Son, whom He has appointed heir of all things, through whom also He made the worlds;*

> *who being the brightness of His glory and the
> express image of His person, and upholding all
> things by the word of His power, when He had
> by Himself purged our sins, sat down at the right
> hand of the Majesty on high,*
>
> *having become so much better than the angels,
> as He has by inheritance obtained a more excel-
> lent name than they.*

Jesus was the brightness of the glory of God, and He entered His destiny by inheritance as the Son of God. To fully step into that destiny on Earth, Jesus had to declare it, as we read in Luke 4:16–21. Following His forty days of temptation in the wilderness, Jesus went into the synagogue, opened the scroll to the Messianic prophecy found in Isaiah 61, and declared eight profound words: *"Today this Scripture is fulfilled in your hearing"* (Luke 4:21).

Jesus knew that it took the power of declaration to transfer promises from the spiritual realm to the earthly realm. In John 16:14, He taught this same principle to His disciples—*"[The Holy Spirit] will glorify Me, for He will take of what is Mine and declare it to you."* If we want something spiritual to occur on Earth, we must declare it.

When Gabriel visited Mary before Jesus was born, he didn't come with mealy-mouthed words. He didn't give his incredible prophetic word weakly: "Um, I was, um, sent by God, and I think He wants to overshadow you. Is that okay? I think He may want you to have a baby. I know you're not married, and we discussed that in heaven. We think you might be strong enough to handle the criticism that will come, but we'll, like, pray with you. Okay?" Gabriel arrived and declared the word of the Lord into being: "I have been in heaven, and you are highly favored there. You are one of God's girls! All of the angels know you. Moses and everyone else know you because you are highly favored. God said He will overshadow you, you will have a baby, and that child will save the world. Nothing is impossible with God!" Gabriel's declaration stirred Mary to the point where she declared her willingness to accept this prophecy. "Let it be," she replied.

When we agree and proclaim what God has declared over us, His word will come to pass, as we read in Isaiah 55:10–12:

> *For as the rain comes down, and the snow from heaven, and do not return there, but water the earth, and make it bring forth and bud, that it may give seed to the sower and bread to the eater,*
>
> *so shall My word be that goes forth from My mouth; it shall not return to Me void, but it shall accomplish what I please, and it shall prosper in the thing for which I sent it.*
>
> *For you shall go out with joy, and be led out with peace; the mountains and the hills shall break forth into singing before you, and all the trees of the field shall clap their hands.*

God is declaring that we will become a generation of unity, intimacy, and maturity. What will your response to Him be?

UNITY

None of us could have progressed to where we are spiritually without the influence and help of other Christians. Growing up, I hated church. Yet I somehow knew God was looking out for me. Somehow, I just knew things that were going to happen; I could sense when danger was imminent.

Growing up as a member of the African-American community, it was not unusual to become involved in the study of the nation of Islam. For almost two years, I wholeheartedly embraced Islamic doctrine, praying five times daily, learning the Koran. Then one day things began to change. I woke up one morning with a question resonating in my spirit: "Has Allah ever answered any of your prayers?" Looking back, I know now that this was the Holy Spirit challenging me. However, at that time I knew nothing of the ways of the Spirit. I was just a guy pondering an important question in his room.

"No," I answered myself.

"Well, it makes no sense to keep talking to somebody who doesn't talk back," the Holy Spirit whispered to me.

Later that day, I asked one of my friends if Allah had ever answered any of his prayers.

"Is he supposed to?" he asked.

That was the day I left my pursuit of Islam for good. I went back to being a full-fledged sinner—in both Muslim and Christian terms. About a year later, I had an encounter that I will never forget. I was lying on my bed looking up at the ceiling when it seemed to disappear. Then, a ball of fire seemed to fall out of the sky into my room and turned into the shape of a man of fire. "I am the Lord Jesus," the Man told me.

Jesus invaded my life that day and introduced Himself to me. He revealed to me things I had done over the previous twenty years. He showed me three occasions where He delivered me from the angel of death. He took me back to each of those experiences and showed me how angelic forces covered and hid me. He even reminded me of what I was thinking in those moments— how arrogant and foolish I was to think I was in control of anything.

In the encounter, Jesus showed me a vision of an elderly gentleman whom I should speak to. At that time, still fresh from the Islamic training, I didn't understand Christianity and considered the Bible to be a "white man's" book (containing only that which would be received by the white race). God even addressed that innermost thought. "It's not about being a white man's book or a black man's book," Jesus said. "I am the 'right' Man for you to get 'right' with." In the days that followed, I didn't tell anyone about the visitation. I really didn't know what to do about that which I had experienced and even questioned if it truly happened! I just knew that I had to find and talk to the elderly gentleman Jesus had shown me.

Two weeks after my encounter, I saw him standing near a water fountain in my neighborhood. Before I could tell him what had happened, this stranger told me exactly what had transpired in the intimacy of my encounter with Jesus. That moment I was brought into the belief of those things of the kingdom of God.

God has continually used other believers to shape my walk with Him. Sometime after my meeting with this elderly gentleman, a friend called me to invite me to what was a start-up ministry with Rick Joyner at the time, which would later become MorningStar Ministries. Before he could even complete his sentence, I answered "No!"

About a minute later, he called again.

"Come," he said.

"No," I replied, hanging up.

Then the phone rang a third time. As I reached out to pick it up, I heard the internal voice of the Spirit say to me, "I want you to go."

I picked up the phone. "Brother," said my friend, "I ain't trying to disrespect you, but the Lord wants you to...."

"I know!" I shouted. "I know I have to go with you!"

"Did the Lord tell you that?" he asked me.

"Yeah," I said.

"He made me call three times, but I told Him that if He didn't speak to you, I wasn't going to keep calling," he laughed.

After the session, Rick Joyner invited several of us to sit down in a circle of chairs with him. As we talked, I heard God say to me, "These are the spiritual knights you are going to join yourself to."

"They don't look like spiritual knights," I replied.

"You don't look like one, either," said God.

God had taken me out of my religious and cultural comfort zones and made me reliant on other people. Over the next two years, as I struggled with how I fit into that place, He worked on my heart and attitude. I learned the importance of working with Christians of every background and experience.

Unity is vital to the success of the body of Christ. As believers, we must stay close to God and we must stay close to one another. It is a simple truth that the enemy uses the same old trick, over and over again, to disrupt us when God is moving: the spirit of division. It distracts and demoralizes us.

The enemy has been planting division in the church for generations. It is easy for most Christians to hear something new, to get excited for a vision, and to say yes to it at first. But then the enemy kicks into high gear, trying to disrupt the flow and formation of what God wants to do. Our relationships with one another must be stronger than the pull of division.

In Daniel 2, as Nebuchadnezzar's soldiers moved to execute wise men throughout the empire for failing to interpret their king's dream, Daniel did not retreat or isolate. He didn't hide by himself. Instead, he went to the king and asked for one night to pray. He gathered his three most trusted friends, Shadrach, Meshach, and Abednego, *"that they might seek mercies from the God of heaven concerning this secret, so that Daniel and his companions might not perish with the rest of the wise men of Babylon"* (Daniel 2:18). What happened? God showed them the way.

It reminds me of the disciples waiting in the upper room. Most of us know the passage well:

When the Day of Pentecost had fully come, they were all with one accord in one place.

And suddenly there came a sound from heaven, as of a rushing mighty wind, and it filled the whole house where they were sitting.

Then there appeared to them divided tongues, as of fire, and one sat upon each of them.

And they were all filled with the Holy Spirit and began to speak with other tongues, as the Spirit gave them utterance
(Acts 2:1-4).

"One accord in one place"—this is the model set out in Scripture for us to follow, especially in moments where the enemy is moving forces against us.

When Nebuchadnezzar built his idol of gold and ordered the nation to worship it, Daniel's three friends stood together against the king. This decision was going to cost them everything. Nebuchadnezzar had decreed that anyone who didn't bow would be thrown in a fiery furnace. In another famous passage of Scripture, we see that their unity in standing for God was rewarded:

Then King Nebuchadnezzar was astonished; and he rose in haste and spoke, saying to his counselors, "Did we not cast three men bound into the midst of the fire?" They answered and said to the king, "True, O king."

"Look!" he answered, "I see four men loose, walking in the midst of the fire; and they are not hurt, and the form of the fourth is like the Son of God" (Daniel 3:24–25).

The unity of those three young men in the face of incredible testing brought the manifest presence of God to their rescue.

UNITY CAN BE CHALLENGING

As you undoubtedly already know, unity with other believers does not always come easily. Daniel and his friends were in bondage in a foreign country, giving counsel to an evil king. The disciples were totally lost in the days after Jesus left them.

All of us have a story and journey in God. Building unity means being interested and involved in one another's walk. Think of the bad situations that have happened in your life that God could have protected you from. He could have altered the course of history in the blink of an eye to spare you that difficulty. In His wisdom, God allows what He could easily prevent by His power. God uses life's circumstances to make us more like Jesus. He allows these things to expose and change our hearts. Through tough moments and issues, we grow in love, perspective, and insight.

I have been known to complain to God about some of the things He has told me to do and some of the obstacles I have faced. However, the Lord continually reminds me of something He told me a few years ago: "Aaron, I have not left it up to chance for anyone to determine their destiny. I have already determined what you are called to do. I have already prepared a place for you. I have written your resume out for you. All you have to do is trust and follow Me."

THE NEW HAMPSHIRE MOVE

How did a ministry overseer like me ever end up working with John Paul Jackson in New Hampshire? Long before I had ever considered joining Streams Ministries, my friend Anna had a dream in which Bob Jones and I were taking a bus from Orlando to New

Hampshire. In the dream, Anna asked me why we were taking a bus and not a plane. "Bob wants to take the bus," I answered matter-of-factly. At that moment, Anna heard the Lord say, "When Aaron goes to New Hampshire, you will need to pray for him."

When Anna phoned me about the dream, I had no intention of moving to New Hampshire. I had visited Streams a couple of times and wondered, "Who could ever live in a place like this?" I had nicknamed the little town "Mayberry" because it was so different from Orlando. A short while after Anna's dream, I had my own encounter with God in which He told me to move north. "Go up there because I will teach you something," He told me. "I'll fast forward you."

For me, the process of being mentored by the Lord and then learning things from an international prophetic leader was exciting. One of the ways of God will teach and train us is by example. The mentoring process is found throughout the Bible. You will find your mentor by the leading of the Holy Spirit. You must learn how to glean and receive from your mentor without interrupting them or their current assignment. Being mentored gives us the opportunity to be fruitful and successful.

What is a mentor? A mentor is an experienced teacher, role model, or counselor who is willing to directly or indirectly impart truths, life experiences, wisdom, and understanding into the lives of others. We can imitate their principles and lifestyles of faith, but not their personalities. They must have a quality or virtue worth pursuing.

Not all mentors are fathers, and we need more fathers in this season. *"He will also go before Him in the spirit and power of Elijah, to turn the hearts of the fathers to the children and the disobedient to the wisdom of the just, to make ready a people prepared for the Lord"* (Luke 1:17). Note that spirit, power, wisdom, and being just are virtues a mentor/father should have.

We all learn from others. Just as people saw the potential in me and mentored me, so I want to help others reach their destinies. When we all enter the fullness of our call, unity becomes easy. I may not have a lot of financial investments, but I have a lot spiritually. I am investing in others to make them great. I can't tell you about stocks and bonds, but I can tell you about spiritual inheritance.

I want to be a part of a holy alliance that desires to live and cultivate the spirit of unity. I want to help facilitate regional prophetic roundtables that network with one another to discover the will of God for every corner of this country. We should all want to be part of the unity of the Spirit—forgetting church wars, church splits, racism, gender issues, and other covenant breaking issues.

God wants to restore the unity of the Spirit and the bond of peace. The Emerging Daniel Company is vital to this restoration. He wants us to have the watchers and the wise see what is coming to disrupt our unity, what is coming to stop us from accessing our destinies, and what is stopping us from being righteous. Wisdom builds the house of God, and knowledge of Him fills it. We must become wise and discerning. We must build with spiritual discernment like Nehemiah.

ANGER: UNITY'S ENEMY

Nothing dismantles unity faster than anger. These days are too important to waste time by nurturing anger. God has too much for this Daniel Company to accomplish. If you are feeling angry, you need to make a conscious choice to shift it into frustration. It is okay to be frustrated; frustration is just a sign of being hungry for something that we can't articulate. We don't know how to process what we are feeling, so we become frustrated.

There is a fine line between frustration and anger, but one is helpful and the other is not. We can often sense that God wants to do something, but we are lost in how to accomplish it. This usually reveals itself as frustration. If we start striving or relying on our flesh to get something done, we short-circuit what God wants to do. Division begins to creep in as people around us are forced to choose between our will and God's plan. This then creates anger and resentment on a number of sides. But if we stay in the Spirit with our frustration, it can change into hunger until revelation comes. "Oh, change this," God may whisper. "Turn this up. Tune this out."

Anger appears when we lose hope, are disappointed in some way, or our expectations have not been met. While God wants us to be passionate and zealous, He wants us to turn away from anger. Anger locks us down, and we cannot open ourselves to others. The moment the lockdown occurs, angels can no longer help us. We have turned our guns on ourselves—we become wounded by our own fire. We have switched the stoker in our lives, choosing to stir our own fire rather than letting God lead us through passion for Him. Anger leaves us in charge of ourselves.

I have spent many seasons of my life in frustration, but that season can change in an instant. My father left me at an early age, and I carried anger against him as a result. That anger and disappointment followed me all of my life until the night God touched me in a dream. I released my dad from anger the day I realized that much of my spiritual gift was inherited from his bloodline. We all need to have bloodline sins cleansed. Exodus 20:5 tells us that sin goes to the third and fourth generation. It is broken and cleansed by the Blood of the Lamb and the Word of God. It is the Luke 4:18 ministry of Jesus.

The finger of God can touch our hearts at any moment and remove years of anger. We just have to repent and ask Him to do it. We can't fool Him anyway: He knows how we feel deep inside. We might as well come clean and work to preserve our unity with His other children.

THE FRUIT OF UNITY

Together, our clean and pure spirits can create atmospheres where we can touch God corporately. As believers who have the Spirit of God within us, we should know what God is going to do when we come together. Sometimes, we let the box of "churchliness" hold back what we need to do in unity. Scripture is clear about God's expectations for our times together:

> *How is it then, brethren? Whenever you come together, each of you has a psalm, has a teaching, has a tongue, has a revelation, has an interpretation. Let all things be done for edification* (1Corinthians 14:26).

We are all contributors to the spiritual environment around us. That's why unity is so important in these end times.

The priestly prayer of Jesus found in John will be fulfilled. *"And the glory which You gave Me I have given them, that they may be one just as We are one"* (John 17:22). "As one" is the prophetic proclamation of this emerging generation of Daniels.

INTIMACY

The Emerging Daniel Company will be marked by its intimacy with the Lord. That was what marked Daniel, and in order for us to come into His fullness, it will be what marks us. Our love for God will and must exceed our love of working for Him. It is this intimacy that the church of Ephesus lacked when they were corrected in Revelation 2:2–4:

> *"I know your works, your labor, your patience, and that you cannot bear those who are evil. And you have tested those who say they are apostles and are not, and have found them liars;*

and you have persevered and have patience, and have labored for My name's sake and have not become weary.

Nevertheless I have this against you, that you have left your first love."

God is challenging us to go back to our first love. We know we have left that first love when we spend more time in our work or ministry than we do with the Lord. Busyness continually takes us away from our first love. It is easy for ministers to equate working *for* God to being *with* God. It's not the same thing! Too many Christians are beguiled by working for God rather than spending time in His presence. God wants us to restore our first love by cherishing His presence in our lives. He then wants others to experience that love we feel.

What distracts you from spending time with God? What disturbs your time in His presence? Individually, we each have to contend for time with God. We need to ask God to teach us how to abide in His presence. This is the single most powerful form of spiritual warfare in our lives today. The greatest war is inside us; it is dealing with our own issues. To be a worshipping warrior who gets prayers answered, we have to first deal with our own issues and, like Daniel, learn how to rest in the Lord. Very few Christians find it easy to simply rest in the Lord. Most of us fight restlessness, boredom, distraction, and a dozen other hindrances. Daniel had favor with man because he first built favor with God by resting in Him. In Daniel 6:10, we read that the prophet made time for God: *"And in his upper room, with his windows open toward Jerusalem, he knelt down on his knees three times that day, and prayed and gave thanks before his God, as was his custom since early days."*

I am at my best in ministry when I am rested. When I have spent time with God, I am sharp. I know what to do, because I am sensitive to His voice. When I have been worshipping, I flow better. David said it best in Psalm 27:4: *"One thing I have desired of the LORD, that will I seek: that I may dwell in the house of the LORD all the days of my life, to behold the beauty of the LORD, and to inquire in His temple."* God wants to teach us how to abide in His presence. This experience is where intimacy with Him is formed.

KNOWING THE SPIRIT, NOT THE FLESH

Another important part of intimacy with the Lord is relying on Him for spiritual food. In the information age we live in, it is easy to read everything, listen to everyone, and get puffed up by knowledge, as Paul put in I Corinthians 8:1. But what God wants us to do can be found in 2Corinthians 5:16: *"Therefore, from now on, we regard no one according to the flesh. Even though we have known Christ according to the flesh, yet now we know Him thus no longer."*

When we are in the presence of God, we don't look at others in the flesh; we see them in the Spirit. I used to test people on this at conferences. If my picture wasn't in the conference brochure, I would show up the first night in a Michael Jordan track suit and Nikes. I would just walk in and sit down. The looks I got would tell me what condition people were in. I saw a lot of, "he must be the janitor" stares. People would walk past me to other leaders until they saw me upfront preaching. Suddenly they would want to talk to me and get prayer from me. Believers should be better than that! We shouldn't be cultural Christians, only seeing in the flesh.

It takes intimacy with God to learn who people are in the Spirit. Communion is an important part of that learning process. I remember one meeting where Bob Jones pointed an elderly woman out to me.

"That grandma's got more relationship with God than all of us sitting on the front row," he said.

When I asked her for prayer afterwards, she prophesied what I was doing, pointing out that I had almost left my first love. She told me I was spending more time in ministry than with the Lord.

"You're wrestling with stuff in your mind," she said. "You've given more thought to the past than the present. Don't you know when God put the blood on it, boy, it don't exist no more! The enemy wants to keep you back there because God has given you a renewed mind, and he doesn't want you to walk in it."

Grandma wasn't a speaker but she knew the word of the Lord. She was not intimidated by what she saw in the flesh for she knew what she saw in the Spirit.

Whenever I ask Him, God has been faithful in showing me who people are in the Spirit. The key to this is found in Romans 8:5-6:

> *For though you might have ten thousand instructors in Christ, yet you do not have many fathers; for in Christ Jesus I have begotten you through the gospel.*
>
> *Therefore I urge you, imitate me.*
>
> *For this reason I have sent Timothy to you, who is my beloved and faithful son in the Lord, who will remind you of my ways in Christ, as I teach everywhere in every church.*
>
> *Now some are puffed up, as though I were not coming to you.*
>
> *But I will come to you shortly, if the Lord wills, and I will know, not the word of those who are puffed up, but the power.*
>
> *For the kingdom of God is not in word but in power.*

As our human spirits are expanded and enlarged, we increase our spiritual sensitivity. Paul knew who was walking with God and who was simply relying on head knowledge. We can too, thanks to the same Holy Spirit who lives in us. When we focus our desire on Jesus, His powerful presence purifies our hearts and brings revelation of His truth and love for others.

PROPHETIC WORSHIP: THE HOLY OBSESSION

God is raising up a multicultural generation of prophetic worshippers, ones who will shine with the beauty and glory of the Lord. The revelation of spirit and science and the creative arts are being opened up. In these arenas, heaven calls us to model lifestyles that encounter the Father and build His house.

When we host the Holy Spirit in corporate settings and are open and available to His direction and immediate witness, we perceive things. We encounter God at levels beyond human reasoning, because we aren't focused on human reasoning but on His Spirit.

Prophetic worship — singing, speaking, or acting under the inspiration of the Spirit of the Lord — is not new. The Psalms are full of prophetic worship.

There are three simple requirements of becoming a prophetic worshipper: intimacy with God; a meditative, contemplative lifestyle; and a hunger and passion to know Him. We need to develop and nurture an intense, holy obsession, because when that happens, we will be changed forever. Cultivating our spirit to wait on Him and being in His presence causes our hearts to become sensitive and enables our dependence on growing in Him. As we learn to follow the Holy Spirit, our spirit grows in the knowledge of God. Encountering God means experiencing His character, and the attributes of God reveals His character. His reality becomes more real and tangible.

When we worship prophetically, it affects the atmosphere; which is sensed and perceived by those present. They understand the message on God's heart. The frequency of the Spirit of God is real, and there are sounds and words found there.

Beholding God's emotions is something only you can do in your own secret life in God. Jesus said that His sheep know His voice (John 10:27). In prophetic worship, we depend upon the voice of God; it is our lifeline. We are becoming lovesick worshippers who adore and worship Him and cultivate atmospheres where heavenly beings and angels feel at home. Heaven is full of this atmosphere that creates new songs.

> *"And they sang a new song, saying: 'You are worthy to take the scroll, and to open its seals; for You were slain, and have redeemed us to God by Your blood out of every tribe and tongue and people and nation,*
> *And have made us kings and priests to our God: And we shall reign on the earth"'* (Revelation 5:9-10).

DECLARATION OF WAR

Worshippers know instinctively that their worship declares war on the enemy. Under the leadership of the Holy Spirit, we focus on loving God. The natural outflow of that intimacy is a brutal assault on the enemy. Intercessors must become addicted to the presence of the Lord. God is taking away all of the hurts, wounds, and disappointments, and replacing them with one desire: *Come on—love Me again.* In intercession, we touch God's heart. We meet Him, greet Him, and entreat Him for His favor. "Do it, as only You can, God," we pray. "You know how to turn this situation around."

God's first call to us is to carry His presence. If we don't have that, we are just like everyone else. We talk loud and say nothing. But intercessors and worshippers who have His presence with them can change the spiritual atmosphere anywhere.

Worship, put simply, is agreeing with who God is, while intercession is agreeing with what God wants to do. Both ways, it starts and ends with the presence of God. They work hand in hand; I do not believe you can have one without the other. No experience on earth can compare with worshipping God. It is all about agreement—recognizing how wonderful, how marvelous, how extravagant and how holy God is. We simply speak out what the four living creatures and the twenty-four elders who sit around the throne in heaven see every day.

God is moving His worshippers from the back row to the front seats. It is time for the creative people among us to stir up the atmosphere and bring the kingdom to earth. We need worshippers to create an environment where the angelic, the prophetic, the creative, and the miraculous can flow. These intimate lovers of God, these residents of the House of the Watchful, these members of the Emerging Daniel Company, are needed to lead us into the presence of God. We all need to be transparent in our worship.

A few years ago, I was set to preach at a church but didn't have a message ready. I kept asking the Lord what He wanted to say, but He kept putting me off. "I'll tell you when you get there," He said. After four songs, I still had nothing. On the fifth song, God spoke to me.

"Write down the titles of the songs you've been singing," He said. "Here is the title of your message: Worship Brings Transparency."

That night, I literally preached from the transparencies of the songs we used to worship God. I led the group through the words of each song and probed as to whether we really meant what we were singing. It is easy to sing, "I surrender all," until God asks you to actually do it. Singing it is a lot easier than living it. "I'll never know how much it cost to see my sin up on that cross" is a statement that is almost impossible to live up to. Yet we sing it almost frivolously.

The Emerging Daniel Company worshippers take intimacy with God very seriously. We continue to develop our spirit to reach that place of ministering to an audience of One. Our songs, our art, our dance, our writing, our banners, our paintings—no matter its form, our worship points to God—and God alone. Intimacy and fellowship help us to learn His voice. Knowing Him is the goal and the prize.

MATURITY

Unity with one another and intimacy with God inevitably lead to the third dominant element in the Emerging Daniel Company believer's life: maturity. As our spirit man expands, our spiritual sensitivity enlarges.

> *Therefore we do not lose heart. Even though our outward man is perishing, yet the inward man is being renewed day by day.*
> *For our light affliction, which is but for a moment, is working for us a far more exceeding and eternal weight of glory,*
> *while we do not look at the things which are seen, but at the things which are not seen. For the things which are seen are temporary, but the things which are not seen are eternal* (2Corinthians 4:16-18).

Daniel understood the power of the unseen. The more he suffered for the cause of the one true God, the more eternal revelation and encouragement he received. This, in turn, continued to mature him prophetically and spiritually. Character was the basic building block in Daniel's life. Daniel got God's attention by fasting from the king's table, by standing up to the most occult regime on the face of the earth, and by putting his faith ahead of his life. *This is a man I can trust with the mysteries of the universe,* God thought to Himself. Daniel matured. He was faithful in little things at first and continued to be faithful as he was given more and more. In return, Daniel received an impartation: a deposit of the Spirit.

CHARACTER FIRST

The only true measure of maturity is character. I have seen gifting supersede character too many times to be impressed by a revelatory anointing anymore. While I lived in Orlando, I was mentoring a young prophetic man from the Northeast. I worked with him constantly on his character, but the lessons never seemed to sink in. He would have visits from angels, give me accurate words of knowledge, and prophesy powerfully. I remember one word he called me with as I was driving to a conference. I had been torn over what to speak; in fact, I had two sermons in my pocket ready to go.

My young friend called me with a Word. "I saw an angel holding a lamp over you, Aaron, and the Lord said, 'Aaron's a little dull. He needs some light.'" The angel then read out the message I was supposed to speak—which was in my pocket.

It was a very impressive and helpful word. Unfortunately, six months later, his wife divorced him. I'm not impressed with gifts or words or anointing anymore. Neither is God, to be blunt. The only thing we should be impressed by is the David test: "Is this a person after God's own heart?" Daniel was clearly such a man; the angel referred to him as "greatly beloved." We are each called to the same. We are *called* to that level of intimacy. It isn't something God gives to just a special, chosen few, like David and Daniel—it is for all of us.

All kingdom issues are heart issues. Every time God brings us into a promotion in the things of the Spirit, He challenges us to further develop our character. If we make the decision to trust God with everything we have, walking in the midst of fire will not burn us; it will only propel us more fully into our destinies. After Shadrach, Meshach, and Abed-Nego were pulled from the fiery furnace—alive—the king promoted them. They were tested in the fire; if God had not given them favor, they would have been completely destroyed. But give them favor He did, and afterward, what had tried to kill them in the beginning ended up honoring them before all (Daniel 3:29–30).

WALKING AHEAD

Maturity is about taking responsibility for ourselves and walking out the things that God has called us to do. 2Peter 1:5-9 says, *"But also for this very reason, giving all diligence, add to your faith virtue, to virtue knowledge, to knowledge self-control, to self-control perseverance, to perseverance godliness, to godliness brotherly kindness, and to brotherly kindness love. For if these things are yours and abound, you will be neither barren nor unfruitful in the knowledge of our Lord Jesus Christ. For he who lacks these things is shortsighted, even to blindness....*It's time that we grow up. For those led by the Spirit of God are the *mature* sons of God.

The following is an example of having to speak the truth in love, so that growing up in all things into Him occurred.

A few years ago, I visited a church where a pastor asked me if the Lord had shown me anything for his community.

"Well, uh, yeah," I replied.

"What is it?" he asked. I paused for a moment. The Word wasn't a positive one, and I struggled with delivering it. Still, he pressed me until I finally gave in.

"The Lord says you have been crying out for your church to grow," I started.

"I have! That's my number one prayer!"

"But the Lord says He can't grow it," I continued.

The pastor was crushed. "Why? My life is..." he trailed off.

"Oh, no," I said. "There's nothing wrong with your life. But the Lord told me that you have too many twenty-year-old babies in the crib; there isn't any room for new ones. You have kept your people as babies in Christ and there is no room in the crib. God will not put newborns in with rusty, twenty-year-old infants."

"What should I do?" he asked.

We are commissioned to equip the saints. The Greek word for *"equipping"* found in Ephesians 4:12 is *katartisismos* meaning to make fit and implying a process and leading to consummation. It is a fitting or preparing fully, and perfecting it is to be fully furnished.

It hurts sometimes to learn the lessons of spiritual maturity, but it is absolutely vital to our future.

> *The ear that hears the rebukes of life*
> *Will abide among the wise.*
> *He who disdains instruction despises his own*
> *soul,*
> *But he who heeds rebuke gets understanding.*
> *The fear of the LORD is the instruction of wisdom,*
> *And before honor is humility*
> (Proverbs 15:31-33).

To become an overcoming generation, we must cooperate with heaven's agenda. We have to shake off the issues that plague us and say, "Hey! I'm growing up and moving on with this stuff!" It is called putting off the old man and being renewed in the spirit of our minds.

WEIGHING OUR WORDS

Mature believers don't fall easily into traps that people with ambitious spirits sometimes create. Most of us who have been around the prophetic for any length of time have had to deal with these ambitious people.

They want so badly to have a significant prophetic word that they simply begin manufacturing them.

I have received ludicrous e-mails from people offering "prophetic" words. Someone once sent me a word calling on Christians to make love to angels. Are you crazy? People say things with no understanding at all; they allow a spirit of perversion and ambition to consume them. For this reason, the prophetic ministry needs to be cleansed and purified. We need God's wisdom more today than ever before. We need His Spirit of Truth to bear witness to what other people say.

There is a level of discernment that comes with spiritual maturity. Mature Christians keep the Bible front and center in their lives. They are intercessors who know and love the purity of the Lord. The spirits of those in the Daniel Company resonate as they move into the presence of God. They understand that every gift in their lives comes from the hand of God Himself, through His mercy; they embrace humility because they know that they can give to God only what came from His hand in the first place.

When God sent me to Orlando to plant a work there, I argued with Him.

"I can't do it," I said.

"Yes, you can," He answered.

"No, I can't," I shot back.

"Great," He said. "Don't take any of My credit when it works."

This concept can be very difficult to grasp, because it goes against our cultural understanding of life. To truly comprehend it takes hours and hours of intimacy with the Spirit of God. As David proclaimed before his people:

> *"Who am I, and who are my people, that we should be able to offer so willingly as this? For all*

things come from You, and of Your own we have given You" (1Chronicles 29:14).

The prophetic voices that I know are grounded in scripture and have a balance of the Word and the Spirit, operating in their lives. In Hebrews 6:1 it says, *"therefore leaving the discussion of the elementary principles of Christ, let us go on to perfection (maturity).* Neville Johnson states that this generation is going to experience the greatest acceleration of personal spiritual growth ever recorded in history.

To the mature, there is hidden wisdom that has been ordained by God before the world for our glory. To the mature, the Spirit reveals the deep things of God. The Spirit teaches them and compares spiritual things with spiritual. The spiritually mature discern and spiritually judge all things. Knowing the mind of the Lord, they can come together in unity and purity of heart and purpose to access the manifold wisdom of Ephesians 3:10.

As shining ones, we as Daniels must live lives that emphasize obedience. In the Book of Daniel, we see the rewards for serving Him and obeying Him in every situation, even if it is difficult and goes against the flow of the culture. Daniel and the three Hebrew boys were rewarded as found in the following accounts in the Book of Daniel:

> *As for these four young men, God gave them knowledge and skill in all literature and wisdom; and Daniel had understanding in all visions and dreams.*
>
> *Now at the end of the days, when the king had said that they should be brought in, the chief of the eunuchs brought them in before Nebuchadnezzar.*
>
> *Then the king interviewed them, and among them all none was found like Daniel, Hananiah,*

Mishael, and Azariah; therefore they served before the king.

And in all matters of wisdom and understanding about which the king examined them, he found them ten times better than all the magicians and astrologers who were in all his realm (Daniel 1:17-20).

Then Nebuchadnezzar was full of fury, and the expression on his face changed toward Shadrach, Meshach, and Abed-Nego. He spoke and commanded that they heat the furnace seven times more than it was usually heated.

And he commanded certain mighty men of valor who were in his army to bind Shadrach, Meshach, and Abed-Nego, and cast them into the burning fiery furnace.

Then these men were bound in their coats, their trousers, their turbans, and their other garments, and were cast into the midst of the burning fiery furnace.

Therefore, because the king's command was urgent, and the furnace exceedingly hot, the flame of the fire killed those men who took up Shadrach, Meshach, and Abed-Nego.

And these three men, Shadrach, Meshach, and Abed-Nego, fell down bound into the midst of the burning fiery furnace.

Then King Nebuchadnezzar was astonished; and he rose in haste and spoke, saying to his counselors, "Did we not cast three men bound into the midst of the fire?" They answered and said to the king, "True, O king."

"Look!" he answered, "I see four men loose, walking in the midst of the fire; and they are not hurt, and the form of the fourth is like the Son of God."

Then Nebuchadnezzar went near the mouth of the burning fiery furnace and spoke, saying, "Shadrach, Meshach, and Abed-Nego, servants of the Most High God, come out, and come here." Then Shadrach, Meshach, and Abed-Nego came from the midst of the fire.

And the satraps, administrators, governors, and the king's counselors gathered together, and they saw these men on whose bodies the fire had no power; the hair of their head was not singed nor were their garments affected, and the smell of fire was not on them.

Nebuchadnezzar spoke, saying, "Blessed be the God of Shadrach, Meshach, and Abed-Nego, who sent His Angel and delivered His servants who trusted in Him, and they have frustrated the king's word, and yielded their bodies, that they should not serve nor worship any god except their own God! (Daniel 3:19-28).

So the king gave the command, and they brought Daniel and cast him into the den of lions. But the king spoke, saying to Daniel, "Your God, whom you serve continually, He will deliver you."

Then a stone was brought and laid on the mouth of the den, and the king sealed it with his own signet ring and with the signets of his lords, that the purpose concerning Daniel might not be changed.

Now the king went to his palace and spent the night fasting; and no musicians were brought before him. Also his sleep went from him.

Then the king arose very early in the morning and went in haste to the den of lions.

And when he came to the den, he cried out with a lamenting voice to Daniel. The king spoke, saying to Daniel, "Daniel, servant of the living God, has your God, whom you serve continually, been able to deliver you from the lions?"

Then Daniel said to the king, "O king, live forever!

My God sent His angel and shut the lions' mouths, so that they have not hurt me, because I was found innocent before Him; and also, O king, I have done no wrong before you."

Now the king was exceedingly glad for him, and commanded that they should take Daniel up out of the den. So Daniel was taken up out of the den, and no injury whatever was found on him, because he believed in his God (Daniel 6:16-23).

The shining ones are grounded in love, faith, and truth. Being filled with the Spirit allows for complete commitment to His ways and His voice, yielding continuous control and consciously claiming daily our allegiance to His Lordship. Learning to submit to the process is key to realizing where you are in your prophetic destiny; growing in favor, authority, influence, increasing in spiritual sensitivity to the Spirit and in revelatory insights in order to strengthen others during these perilous times. Further, encouraging, equipping, and empowering those who are calling on the God of heaven for guidance, help, and direction. *"Good and upright is the Lord; therefore He instructs sinners in the way. He leads the humble in justice, and He teaches the humble His way* (Psalm 25:8-9).

The shining ones as stars are being aligned by the Son. Those who are wise shall shine like the brightness of the firmament, and those who turn many to righteousness like the stars forever and ever (Daniel 12:3). The shining ones know that it is essential that we have the spirit of understanding so that we can understand the times.

CHAPTER THREE

UNDERSTANDING THE TIMES

In order to get a sense for where we are at, we need to take a look at what we (the Western World) have just come through. Reflecting upon the past decade (2000-2009), we could call it 'the decade that changed the world'.

2000 The Bush/Cheney presidential election which ignited a call for reformation of the electoral ballot system in the State of Florida; then, in

2001 We experienced the tragedy of September 11th.

2002-3 The destruction of the World Trade Centers and attack on our Pentagon led to the decision to enter Iraq.

2003 At the close of this year, Saddam Hussein was captured.

2004 Ronald Reagan, the 40th president of the United States passed away.

2005 marked the deaths of Pope John Paul II as well as Rosa Louise McCauley Parks, who was a pioneer of the Civil Rights Movement.

2006 Our 38th president, Gerald Ford, passed away.

2007 On January 4, Nancy Pelosi became first female speaker of the House of Representatives. This shift in the political arena continued.

2008 Yet again, another memorable presidential election with Barack Obama and Sarah Palin in the race.

2009 The first Hispanic Supreme Court Justice, Sonia Sotomayor, assumed office and Ted Kennedy, known as "the liberal lion" passed away marking the end of a dynasty.

Now as we enter 2010, I believe that we are in the most important and Biblically relevant time of human existence as it relates to "the times of the end."

THE CALLING FORTH OF THE ISSACHAR ANOINTING

We must first set our hearts to understand as Daniel did (Daniel 10:12). The humbling of ourselves and setting the heart is a lifestyle that must be cultivated. In Matthew 16:3, the Lord rebuked the spiritual leaders for not being able to discern the signs of the times. In Matthew 24:3-8, the disciples asked Jesus three questions that pertained to timing. The questions were: Tell us (the emerging leaders) when will these things be? What will be the sign of Your coming? What will be the sign of the end of the age?

First, they are warned not to be deceived. Jesus then goes on to talk about wars and rumors of wars. Nation will rise against nation, and kingdom against kingdom. We are all familiar with the Holocaust, but few are aware of the genocide that took place shortly before World War I. In 1913 in the Middle East, one million Christian Armenians were massacred by the Turks. One million believers killed and hardly anybody knows or talks about it. For more information I recommend the book, *The Armenians: From Kings and Priests to Merchants and Commissars,* by Razmik Panossian. For a better understanding of Matthew 24 and 25, I would highly suggest that you read and study Derek Prince's book, *Prophetic Guide to the Endtimes: Facing the Future Without Fear.*

There is a major confrontation coming with the realms of darkness, and we need to be prepared as Daniel was. According to Daniel 12, the prophet envisioned a glorious end that saw the God of heaven having complete victory over evil and things being restored. However, it did not come without a fight. We are in a prophetic countdown. The kingdom of God is advancing and our time is ticking into His future. Associated with the kingdom advancing is the ability to have understanding. Matthew 13:11-23 states that it is the word of the kingdom that must be understood.

UNDERSTANDING ISSACHAR

Issachar was the ninth son of Jacob and the fifth son of Leah. According to Chuck Pierce in his book, *Interpreting the Times*, Issachar was positioned strategically with Judah and Zebulun (Numbers 2:5, 10:14-15). The tribes were in tremendous conflict and transition. The government was changing from the house of Saul to the house of David. Several characteristics are given concerning Issachar: prosperity, intercession, divine alignment, the ability to ascertain seasonal and immediate changes, understanding of war and political changes, and most importantly how to position himself at the right place at the right time. The Issachar anointing releases the spirit of understanding and insight into what to do and how to do it.

The Issachar anointing will affect and influence those within our economic, governmental, and business infrastructures so that the kingdoms of this world become the kingdoms of our Lord (Revelation 11:15). A new kingdom mindset must be established. This can only come from spending time in His presence, which causes understanding, insight, and strategies to flow. Being saturated with His presence and knowing His voice enables us to be spiritually fine-tuned, receive favor, and walk in the Spirit which is moving in His timing and rhythm. The anointing of recognition from those in the world system will become apparent (Daniel 5:29, 4:18 and Genesis 41:38–39).

We are being empowered to be discerning and wise. God's wisdom and understanding will flow during these dark and turbulent times, and we have authority in the Spirit which comes with understanding and divine wisdom. Both light and darkness are maturing. The sons of the kingdom are about to demonstrate this and advance His purposes as our mindset becomes grounded in kingdom perspective. Our perspective needs to be that His kingdom is designed to take over, not to co-exist with evil. *Darkness will cover the earth and gross darkness the people* (Isaiah 60:2–3), but the Lord will arise over us and His glory will be seen upon us. Understanding His ways and knowing what is about to come upon us is essential.

Unprecedented changes are continuing to occur, and the Lord is orchestrating most of these changes. It is stated God changes the times and the seasons (Daniel 2:21). He schedules the international, national, and individual events in our lives. We must ask the Father what He is doing and what our assignment is in the progressive unfolding of His plan, purpose, and counsel. Having a kingdom perspective connected to the process brings us to a place of alignment and formation that awakens us to His guiding eye.

We are in a time of acceleration. My wife, Jill Marie, and I were traveling in my car in New Hampshire, having been invited by Scott and Barbara Evelyn to minister at the New London Bridge Church—the first Bridge church planted by John Paul Jackson. While driving to have dinner, I noticed the speedometer was at 90 mph.

We were in a 45 mph speed zone. Jill Marie looked over and saw the speedometer indicating close to 100 mph. I let up on the gas, but it still showed close to 100 mph. Needless to say, we were concerned until I heard the Lord's internal voice say "You are now in a season of acceleration and you have no control over it." This was an understatement!

What were we instructed to do? Watch, wait, listen, and cooperate.

We are approaching the Feast of Tabernacles where in the Book of Nehemiah, the book was opened and understanding given. The season we are in is the open book season where we will receive insight and understanding for the times we are in (Daniel 12:4).

The Feast of Tabernacles—the fullness, the Glory, and the rest—that's where we are headed. We will need to be discerning, watchful, and bold in our understanding the times. As the Lord begins to release strategic initiatives to advance His kingdom, we must be alert and sober. Restoration and redemption will reveal solutions that will allow a kingdom culture to be established so that every nation, tribe, and people can experience the Lord of loving-kindness, righteousness, and justice. Understanding that strategic alliances must be made between believers as well as non-believers is essential. Scripture reveals that non-believers like Cyrus and King Hiram in Solomon's time are key people the Lord will use to fulfill His purposes.

Teams who seek and inquire of the Lord for counsel will be established in these times. The Issachars know what to do, but we also need a team that knows the ways of the Lord and the schemes of the enemy. We are in a new era of engagement where all the parts must function as a whole. The new model will experience resistance (Luke 5:37–39). We must understand the old mindsets but not be intimidated by them. The Holy Spirit is weaving together business, media, communications, education, technology, government, and ministries for a great mobilization to affect the harvest. Daniel 2 says that He changes the times and the seasons; He gives wisdom to the wise and knowledge to those who have understanding. In this restoration period, all things are being used for His purposes. A renewed mind and an understanding heart can perceive what the Lord is doing and how best to align with Him.

Right now, nations are in dismay. Regions in our country are suffering economically and socially. Major power shifts are occurring. New alliances for good and for evil are being formed. With all the stirring, shaking, and changes happening, we know and understand that the Lord is in control. There is a wealth transfer to occur. In his book, *The Joseph – Daniel Calling,* Morris E. Ruddick says: "Kingdom opportunities and new mindsets in harmony with God's strategic, redemptive purposes for the wealth transfer will emerge (Proverbs 13:22). Mindsets prepared and poised to respond to God's pivotal agendas for our day as the Josephs and Daniels are mobilized and the opportunities associated with the transfer of wealth begin to be recognized and gain momentum" (page 86).

In the midst of intense darkness and light (the time of the Gentiles ticking down), it is the revelation of God's love towards us that will keep and strengthen us (Daniel 10:11, 18 and Daniel 9:23). Understanding His will is a right perspective about His wisdom, His ways, and His judgments. His wisdom is His strategy—it is understanding why God acts the way He does. His way is understanding what He is doing in human affairs to bring everything under the leadership of His Son.

Understanding the revelation and agreeing with it brings us to a place of submission to His leadership. This is the place we must enter and abide—"*under the shadow of the Almighty*" (Psalm 91:1).

Many shall be purified, made white, and refined, but the wicked shall do wickedly and none of the wicked shall understand; however, the wise shall understand. The impartation of the spirit of understanding shall make us strong and able to carry out great exploits.

We desperately need the Spirit of understanding in these times. We must press into the Lord for this empowerment so that we can lead others and help them avoid being deceived, shipwrecked, or destroyed. Living with understanding will cause light to shine and our hearts to rejoice. Understanding carries discernment, wisdom, and the counsel of the Lord. The Spirit of understanding is transferable and every one of us can cry out for it. Understanding His ways is growing in timing and knowing His perspective. When we have understanding, we flow with the Lord and His purposes. One of the keys to acquiring understanding is to wait on Him and position ourselves to yield to the Spirit of truth. Submission and commitment to Him increases our insight and discernment.

In 1998, I had a prophetic dream about standing on the ten toes of a huge, tall statue. The Holy Spirit spoke to me and said, "Go to Daniel chapter 2." It took years to understand this prophetic dream, but it was a dream from the Lord giving me understanding concerning the time and the primary function of my prophetic destiny. In Daniel 2, the God of heaven outlines the history of the world in much detail and the course of time from Daniel until the second coming of Christ. This is referred to as the times of the Gentiles, and starts from the captivity of Judah and ends with His second coming and establishing of the millennial kingdom age.

God had committed the government of the world to the nation of Israel, administered through priests, prophets, and godly kings; however, the nation became disobedient and God interrupted the kingdom and committed it to the Gentile nations. Standing symbolically on the toes indicates a timing issue. The image and my experience represented the kingdoms and governments of this world, and that during the time of the ten toes, which are ten kings, the Lord will set up His kingdom (Daniel 2:44).

KINGDOM PROMOTION

For exaltation comes neither from the east nor the west nor from the south,

but GOD is the judge: He puts down one, and exalts another (Psalm 75:6-7).

Daniel is a model on how to be promoted by the Lord. He lived a life of loyalty, honor, and excellence which are virtues foreign to the Western church, but very important to the Lord. Loyalty and honor are relational terms and denote an enduring commitment to a person over a period of time. They are mostly associated with relationship to the present leadership over us. Daniel demonstrated loyalty to God in every situation, yet he presented himself to those over him with respect and discretion.

Promotions come because of faithfulness to the Lord and the assignment given by Him. Being loyal to those over us is not synonymous with unqualified allegiance, nor is it being naïve about the leaders' weaknesses. It is cultivated daily by staying in communion with the Spirit who causes us to spiritually appraise what is right.

When we are loyal to the Lord, we do not yield to the fear of men nor are we man-pleasers. The Lord's eyes are said to run to and fro throughout the whole earth, to show Himself strong on behalf of those whose hearts are loyal to Him (2Chronicles 16:9). Loyalty to God is a key to being promoted by Him and having Him display His might and power on your behalf. The three Hebrew boys, Hananiah, Mishael, and Azariah, were loyal in the face of not worshipping the image that Nebuchadnezzar had made (Daniel 3). Loyalty does not bow to cultural pressure or fear. The Lord demonstrates to us that if we do not bow, we will not burn. Daniel was promoted several times, and each time it positioned him to advance the kingdom and give God the glory (Daniel 5:29; Daniel 6:1-2). Living a life that is loyal and honorable strengthens our resolve to walk in a spirit of excellence.

The Emerging Daniel Company is being formed into a company of people who are developing an excellent spirit. *"And this I pray, that your love may abound still more and more in knowledge and all discernment, that you may approve the things that are excellent" (Philippians 1:9-10).* We must increase personal excellence so that we may enhance the corporate excellence needed to manifest God's kingdom.

We pray that an impartation of the seven-fold anointing of Daniel 5:11-12 be upon you for your assignment as you live a life of loyalty and honor before Him. The sevenfold anointing is: the Spirit of the Lord, an excellent spirit, knowledge, understanding, interpreting dreams, solving problems, and explaining enigmas. The Emerging Daniel Company are kingdom consultants who are growing in these anointings.

What time is it? It time to Arise shine for our light has come! And the glory of the Lord is risen upon us. For behold the darkness shall cover the earth and deep darkness the people, But the Lord will arise over you And His glory will be seen upon you. The Gentiles shall come to your light, And kings to the brightness of your rising.

CHAPTER FOUR

KINGDOM CONSULTANTS

W ho are these kingdom consultants? What is their function and what do they do?

We are "Kingdom Solution Providers" (a term coined by David Sellick). We have been in training and growing in spiritual authority, maturity, and godly wisdom for the purpose of being strategically placed alongside those who are in positions of authority—those leaders who are seeking the guidance and counsel of the Lord.

As His ambassadors, we have been equipped to release heaven's perspective for those in the seven strategic mountains of cultural influence (the components that shape our society: education, government, business, family, media, religion/faith, and entertainment). Our supernatural anointing is for the purpose of seeing His perspective administrated in every area of life. As representatives of His kingdom, our counsel is based on His righteousness and justice being established.

During a time of seeking the Lord concerning direction, He began talking to me about the Emerging Daniel Company, formed by 'Kingdom Consultants'. "Kingdom Consultants," I thought. "Yes, do not put President or Director on the business card," He exclaimed. "How strange," I thought. "What will we do and is it biblical?"

Scripturally, the five-fold ministries are consultants. I began to study the life, ministry, gift-mix, and anointing of Daniel including the Spirit of counsel and wisdom, the sevenfold anointing of Daniel (see Daniel 5:11-12), character, faithfulness, being transported (Daniel 7 and 8), spiritual understanding (Daniel 1:20), and loyalty, with the gifting to be a watcher and intercessor. Scripture proves that counselors and consultants were always around, but the kingdom of darkness has occupied this place for a long time. This privileged place of influence is key to advancing the kingdom.

All of us have been created to influence someone or something. Kingdom Consultants are anointed and positioned by the Lord of Hosts to influence kings in each of the seven mountains so that the Lord's agenda can be promoted. They are those who are called to occupy the high places, to release His values, and to establish a kingdom culture.

Jill Marie and I were at Bob and Bonnie Jones' house in November 2008. Bob Hartley and Bob Fraser were also present. Bob Hartley did not know about our ministry but told us that by January 20, 2010, there would be a releasing of the Daniels. He mentioned that this would represent three years for something (this date would represent three years from the date I first met Jill Marie). He had no idea about the name of the ministry or again, who we were or what assignment the Lord had commissioned us to do. If we ever need Daniels, especially in these times and with this present administration, it is now.

Daniels are anointed to solve problems and relate the ways of the Lord. They have the anointing to make the crooked places straight. The Spirit of counsel will empower them to give the counsel of the Lord.

Several years ago, John Sandford and I ministered together. We were taking turns doing the meetings; however, the next morning when it was my turn, the

Lord quickened in my spirit that I was to open up the meeting with the topic of the "Counsel of the Lord," but I was to turn it over to John. I shared this with John and Paula at the hotel before leaving. John jumped up and first said, "What did you say?" I timidly repeated what I said. John looked at me and then at Paula and said that early in the morning the Lord had taken him up to the Counsel of the Lord! He was not sure if he was to share it, so he said to the Lord, "If this is from You Lord, then You'll have to speak to Aaron." At first, I was happy that I had heard the Lord, then the flesh kicked in and I said in my heart, "Lord, You could have taken me up and I could have shared it myself." In an internal, audible voice, the Lord said, "Aaron, it's not your time!" In God's economy, timing is everything (Daniel 5:29). Promotion comes by being trustworthy and obedient. (It was many years later when, Jill-Marie and I visited John Sandford and he revealed that the gift of 'musicality' had been imparted to her and then he blessed me with the ability to access the Counsel of the Lord.)

It all begins with the loyalty test. Being loyal to the King of Kings and dedicated to His purposes will prepare us to stand before earthly kings. Standing before kings is our function, but staying in His presence is our source. The Lord put Daniel in that place of influence. He had experience, wisdom, and leadership, a sense of history, a good reputation, ability, revelation, and a servant's heart. This is the gift mix that Kingdom Consultants must possess.

Kingdom Consultants are transitional coaches, spiritual mentors, and business coaches with proven track records. Their insight and understanding influences others for righteousness. They live by a kingdom code that is grounded in love, truth, and faith. They shine like stars with varying capacities of light to help see and understand how to collaborate with heaven's perspective for the lives of those with whom they partner. They watch what the Father is doing and look for the assignment He's given them to accomplish. Their delight is understanding the process and declaring the decrees of the Lord.

With the understanding that spiritual gates need to be removed, replaced, or reformed, they have spiritual discernment along with the spiritual authority to help at the gates of cities and regions. They work as a team that inquires of the Lord of Hosts for the wisdom that comes from above, concerning the gates and the high places. These Kingdom Solution Providers' passion is to see His kingdom come and His will be done on earth as it is in heaven.

This company of Kingdom Consultants is helping leadership make the transition into the new and journaling how to navigate uncharted waters. They assure arrival into the true apostolic, avoiding deception and humanistic thinking. The government of God must be established by the wisdom and ways of the Lord; discerning between the true and the false. With a multitude of counselors there is safety.

Kingdom Consultants come alongside to help with alignment, assignment, and strategies. Consultants help church and ministry leaders make the shift into kingdom reality and strengthen leaders so that they can prepare the people to make straight the way of the Lord and help them find their God-ordained purposes. Kingdom Consultants provide solutions for leadership so that they have no need to consult with or go to psychics (1Chronicles 10:13–14 and Daniel 2:2, 2:27).

By definition a consultant is one who provides counsel. We have many biblical examples of those who have received the counsel of the Lord for particular people as well as groups of people in the specific spheres of various cultures. Elijah, Elisha, Amos, David, and Daniel are among those individuals who not only provided counsel, but also wisdom, understanding, knowledge, and might.

The Emerging Daniel Company is composed of individuals who will be Kingdom Solution Providers. Their solutions pertain to issues and problems arising from faulty foundations and cultural constructs based on the present "cosmos" or world system. The shining ones of Daniel will be vessels to provide enlightenment, insight, and wisdom for people and institutions that have darkened understanding.

> *There is a man in your kingdom in whom is the Spirit of the Holy God. And in the days of your father, light and understanding and wisdom, like the wisdom of the gods, were found in him; and King Nebuchadnezzar your father—your father the king—made him chief of the magicians, astrologers, Chaldeans, and soothsayers.*
>
> *Inasmuch as an excellent spirit, knowledge, understanding, interpreting dreams, solving riddles, and explaining enigmas were found in this Daniel, whom the king named Belteshazzar, now let Daniel be called, and he will give the interpretation* (Daniel 5:11-12).

The kingdoms of this world are waiting for this company to emerge. The emerging company's estimated time of arrival is 2010-2012.

PRIESTS WITH A KINGLY ANOINTING

Priests with a kingly anointing are an aspect of government. They pursue His presence with passion. Their passion and primary calling is to bring Him pleasure by ministering unto the affections of the Lord. They live a consecrated lifestyle, having their spiritual identity imprinted on their heads as sons, servants, and representatives of the King of Kings. Their function is to demonstrate His kingdom and display His power on earth as it is in heaven.

Priests have a lifestyle of intimacy, cultivating the secret place where strategies flow. Drinking from the well of His presence is their daily delight. They occupy the high places by releasing prophetic declarations that shift the atmosphere and empower the angelic realm and the hosts of heaven. The well of His presence emboldens us with the essences of His substance which displaces the religious spirit and sets the captive free.

Intimacy, purity, and maturity sustain us to live a supernatural lifestyle that glorifies God. Modeling a lifestyle that does not quench or grieve the Holy Spirit causes the realities of heaven to be manifested on earth. As the royal priesthood, we have been given access to His divine presence and the awesome privilege of interacting and communing with the Living God.

A priestly seer company needs to be trained, equipped, and taught concerning the order of Melchizedek (Hebrews 7:17, 24-25). Melchizedek was both a king and a priest. This order will produce a priesthood of believers who minister according to the power of an indestructible life, administered by the Holy Spirit. The priestly order of Melchizedek is the highest priestly order that the Lord has established for His people. It affects the priesthood of the believer in the church and the marketplace. The eternal priestly order empowers spiritual leaders to be involved in a profitable business and a church or ministry, just as Paul was, as we see in Acts 18:1-4.

Under the order of Melchizedek, every believer is in full-time ministry. Ministering unto the Lord will give us access to the wisdom, influence, and favor we need to affect the seven mountains. We are a part of an everlasting priesthood. The foundation of this order is righteousness, according to Hebrews 7:1-2. Melchizedek was king of righteousness, and reigned over the sphere of righteousness. Righteousness is being in right standing with the Lord Himself.

What are some of the benefits of righteousness? Righteousness exalts a nation (Proverbs 14:34); the work of righteousness will be peace, and the effect of righteousness, quietness and assurance forever (Isaiah 32:170); the Lord puts on righteousness as a breastplate (Isaiah 59:17). We are told to put on the breastplate of righteousness as a part of the whole armor of God (Ephesians 6:10-18); the gift of righteousness empowers us to reign in life (Romans 5:17); and presenting our members as instruments of righteousness to God, or put another way, learning to yield to the influence of the Spirit—to be controlled by the Spirit (Romans 6:13). The prophet Ezekiel, in chapter fourteen, uses Daniel as a model of righteousness.

Melchizedek was the King of Salem, which means peace that leads to nothing missing or nothing broken. Peace is an attribute of the Lord. The order of Melchizedek is based on the Lord's divinity. David heard the revelation of Melchizedek hundreds of years before the birth of Christ (Psalm 110:4). Coming under this priestly order will break every generational curse that has been flowing through the bloodlines.

We desperately need clear revelation about the order of Melchizedek. On the horizon is a priestly generation who will function with a kingly anointing. This unchangeable priesthood will empower a generation to wage holy war. Advancing the kingdom and occupying until He comes will be their delight.

As priests minister unto the Lord, it enhances the seeing and hearing realm. Samuel ministered unto the Lord. At first, revelation was rare (1 Samuel 3:1) but in verse 20, all Israel "knew." Revelation increases as we minister to Him. In the Old Testament, most prophets who ministered to Him were priests.

Just as it was in David's reign, I believe God will restore David's tabernacle again. Priestly seers will play a major role in restoring the spirit of the

Tabernacle of David. It was the king and priests who both sought after and soaked in the presence of the Lord so the spiritual inheritance of the people could be manifested. Revelation and the demonstration of heaven's realities are the marks of this priesthood of believers. Seeing in the invisible and speaking with authority releases the word that brings transformation and change

Scripture records nine Seers who were with David during the time of David's administration and Tabernacle:

Samuel	1Chron 29:29	Governmental Advisor
Gad	1Chron 29:29	Governmental Advisor
Zadok	2Sam 15:27	Chief Priest
Hanani	2Chron16:7	Samuel's Grandson
Iddo	2Chron 9:29	Priest
Amos	Amos 7:12	Marketplace
Asaph	2Chron 29:30	Worship Leader
Jeduthun	2Chron 35:15	Worship Leader
Heman	1Chron 25:5	Worship Leader

There are many expressions of this priestly-seer anointing. Among other things, I see the Emerging Daniel Company functioning in three expressions that are most like Daniel himself—governmental (apostolic authority), prophetic intercession and watching.

Standing before the King, passionately pursuing His presence, beholding the beauty of the Lord, carrying His glory, to receive His approval, and to be given the affectionate endorsement of being beloved (Daniel 10:11,19) is worth the sacrifice of a life of consecration, separation, dedication, and commissioning.

Our worship and intercessory function is our primary activity, calling those things that are not as though they were. We can sum it up as a five-fold function:

1. Separating the precious from the vile
2. Demonstrating faithfulness even in the darkest of times
3. Accessing the counsel of the Lord for others
4. Releasing the fragrances of the Lord to infuse life and light
5. Establishing the government of God

The Lion of the tribe of Judah is in the midst of this kingdom and royal priesthood. Revelation 5:5-10 says that the Lion of the tribe of Judah, the Root of David, has prevailed to open the scroll and loose its seven seals. *"And have made us kings and priests to our God. And we shall reign on the Earth."* V. 10

THE "KINGLY MINISTRY"

In Jeremiah 50:41, it says that many kings shall be raised up from the ends of the earth. Kings are leaders in their respective fields.

The Lord is raising up many kings to accomplish His purposes. The kingly anointing is for ruling and reigning. It is an anointing for Apostolic government and breaking through into new territories to advance the Kingdom of God. This kingly anointing wins wars in the realm of the Spirit.

This anointing is accessed by being in the atmosphere of the Tabernacle. The manifest presence activates the Kingly realm. In His presence we are touched by the scepter of the King of Kings to accomplish the impossible. The scepter represents His favor and His authority.

In David Swan's book *The Ministry of Kings* he lists five indispensible roles:

1. Providing decisive leadership
2. Providing clear solutions to problems
3. Accelerating the release of resources

4. Swiftly implementing and executing the plans and purposes of God. And
5. Forming strategic alliances among those with the Kingly ministry for greater global impact.

Biblical kings are anointed and operate from a place of spiritual authority, wisdom and largeness of heart. (Another good book is by Harold R. Eberle and John S. Garfield entitled *Releasing Kings for Ministry in the Marketplace.*)

The marketplace has the potential for an outpouring of the Spirit in the greatest revival that the world has yet to see.

CHAPTER FIVE

KINGDOM AUTHORITY

All four visions God gave to Daniel pertain to future events. Here is a summary of the four visions:

Daniel 7: The first vision was recorded to have taken place in approximately 555 B.C. in the first year of Belshazzar, who incidentally was the last king of Babylon. The revelation includes prophetic insight about the Ancient of Days, the Son of Man, and the dominion, glory, and a kingdom given to Him with the assurance that all people, nations, and languages should serve Him. Further, His dominion is an everlasting dominion (vs. 14) which shall not pass away and His kingdom will be the one which shall not be destroyed.

In Daniel 8, the vision of the ram and the he-goat, Daniel is transported from Babylon to the province of Elam at Shushan, the palace, which was approximately 230 miles away. The ram symbolizes the kings of Media and Persia (8:20). The ram is challenged by a he-goat and defeated by him. In verses 21–22, we are told clearly that the goat was Greece and the great horn symbolizes the first king which was Alexander the Great. Gabriel is sent to give Daniel understanding (vs. 16).

The third vision is found in Daniel 9. It is said to have occurred about 538 B.C. in the first year of the reign of Darius the Mede (Daniel 9:1). Daniel, by prayer, study, and searching the Scriptures, is awakened to the timing of a restoration prophesied in the Book of Jeremiah. Intercession was released and the answer from the throne was delivered (Daniel 9:20–27). Again, Gabriel comes to Daniel to give him skill to understand.

The fourth vision occurs in Daniel 10–12 which gives us a behind-the-scenes revelation about how the nations will be affected by either the host of angels or the network of evil angels. A real conflict exists between the two in the invisible realm. We are given a glimpse of the dark side and their agenda to dominate those in authority for Satan's purpose. Daniel 10:1–3 is the revelation of things to come. Daniel 10:4–9 is the seven-fold revelation of the Lord:

1. Clothed in linen
2. Girded around the waist with gold of Uphaz
3. Body like beryl
4. Face like the appearance of fire
5. Eyes like torches of fire
6. Arms and feet like burnished bronze in color
7. The sound of His words like the voice of a multitude

Daniel is once again told that he is greatly beloved and since the first day he set his heart to understand and humble himself (Daniel 10:11–14).

Daniel progressively grew in Kingdom authority. In Daniel chapters 2, 4, and 5 he interprets the dreams and visions of others. He receives his first recorded visions in chapters 7 and 8. Daniel is transported from one geographic place to another. In chapter 9 he encounters the angel Gabriel who imparts skill to understand, and insight and understanding concerning the future of Israel. In chapter 10 he encounters the Lord Himself.

Like Daniel, we need to grow from interpreting dreams, into supernatural God-ordained transportations and interactions with angels, concerning revelation for kings and nations. We need to encounter the Lord Himself and receive the seven-fold Spirit of God (Revelation 5:6 and Isaiah 11:2, 3) for our times. Daniel 10:10–21 gives us unfolding, divine information from the angelic ministry. The angel touches to release strength, and explains the process and protocol on how things will play out. The angel gives insight into the prince of the kingdom of Persia (which we currently see very active again, operating in and through Iran and their president, Mahmoud Ahmadinejad).The angel closes with the revelation that he will go back to engage in warfare with the evil supernatural being. The battle pertains to the occupation of a place of influence with Persian kings and subsequently, rulers in Greece.

An Emerging Daniel Company is being equipped and anointed with apostolic grace and governmental intercession to participate with heaven and the angelic hosts, to affect places and people of influence so that the gospel of the Kingdom can be preached to all the world and nations (Matthew 24:14).

What is the preaching of the gospel of the Kingdom? It is the declaration of the rule and reign of God over all. It ensures the administration of the government of God, which is the absolute power from which all other powers issue and to which they submit (Colossians 1:13–17, 2:15; Psalm 24:1–2; and Ephesians 1:19–23).

Understanding the influence that the unseen plays behind-the-scenes is essential. Equally important is being prepared to align and flow with the Lord of Hosts to render the prince of this world ineffective in our sphere of influence. The Lord referred to Satan three times as "the prince of this world system" (John 12:31, 14:30, and 16:11). Prince or ruler describes his rank; the power of the air or world system explains his area of domain.

There is a sound of war increasing. Are you dressed for the battle? We must be prepared by being trained and putting on the full armor of God (Ephesians 6:13–15).

We need a new vision of spiritual warfare. Mature sons and daughters must establish regional war councils that access the Lord of Host's counsel and guidance. *"This also comes from the Lord of Hosts who is wonderful in counsel and excellent in guidance"* (Isaiah 28:29).

Divine counsel along with the Spirit of Might will provide continuous expressions of the Spirit of the Lord during these transitional times. A generation of over-comers is arising with kingdom authority. The principle of submission to His Lordship is the key to our being victorious (Romans 14:7–12), in addition to humbling ourselves to be trained and instructed in righteousness and servanthood. The degree to which we demonstrate willingness to submit to Him and serve others will determine the level of authority we will walk in. Walking in the fullness will require total surrender to the leadership of the Holy Spirit. The more we yield the more strength we will receive. Experiencing and knowing how to discern the release of the Spirit comes by learning how to yield to the restraint of the Spirit. Yielding our members to righteousness (Romans 6:13) empowers us to walk in authority and the demonstration of the Spirit. Authority is the legal right to act—kingdom authority is a powerful responsibility that releases the life of heaven into earthly situations. It spiritually aligns things with heaven's purposes so that the light and life of God can be experienced and embraced. John 1:4 says: *"In Him was life, and the life was the light of men."* Light illuminates so that we can see where to go.

Growing in our kingdom authority entails learning and knowing how to use proper keys at the proper time. We have been given and we are in the Kingdom now. Luke 22:28-29 says that because the disciples con-tinued with Him in trials He bestowed a kingdom on them, just as His Father bestowed (conferred) one on Him. Also, Colossians states that He delivered us (that's you and me) from the power of darkness and conveyed us into the kingdom of the Son of His love.

This authority only works when one is under authority. That means we need to be submitted to the Lord and the spiritual government of a local fellowship. KEYS (Kingdom Empowerment for Your Sphere of Influence) operate best in the context of knowing and being with Him and being divinely connected with those of like-mindedness.

Here are some keys we must use to shift and challenge the status quo and invite the invasion of the kingdom of God:

1. **Humility—cultivating a broken heart**
    For thus says the High and Lofty One Who inhabits eternity, whose name is Holy: "I dwell in the high and holy place, with Him who has a contrite and humble spirit, to revive the spirit of the humble, and to revive the heart of the contrite ones" (Isaiah 57:15).

2. **Declarations**
    I have declared the former things from the beginning; they went forth from My mouth, and I caused them to hear it. Suddenly I did them, and they came to pass.
    You have heard; seeing all this will you not declare it? I have made you hear new things from this time, even hidden things, and you did not know them (Isaiah 48:3, 6).

3. **Tongues**
    He who speaks in a tongue does not speak to men but to God, for no one understands him; however, in the Spirit he speaks mysteries (1Corinthians 14:2).

4. **Wisdom from above**

But the wisdom that is from above is first pure, then peaceable, gentle, willing to yield, full of mercy and good fruits, without partiality and without hypocrisy (James 3:17).

5. **Spiritual discernment**

And this I pray, that your love may abound still more and more in knowledge and all discernment (Philippians 1:9).

6. **Watching**

Blessed is the man who listens to me, watching daily at my gates, waiting at the posts of my doors (Proverbs 8:34).

7. **The blood of Jesus**

But if we walk in the light as He is in the light, we have fellowship with one another, and the blood of Jesus Christ His Son cleanses us from all sin (1John 1:7).

And they overcame him by the blood of the Lamb (Revelation 12:11).

8. **Intercession – Warriors of the Spirit**

Therefore I exhort first that supplications, prayers, intercessions, and giving of thanks be made for all men (1Timothy 2:1).

For though we walk in the flesh, we do not war according the flesh. For the weapons of our warfare are not carnal but mighty in God for pulling down strongholds (2Corinthians 10:3-4).

9. **Spirit of revelation and anointing**

(I) do not cease to give thanks for you, making mention of you in my prayers:

that the God of our Lord Jesus Christ, the Father of glory, may give to you the spirit of wisdom and revelation in the knowledge of Him (Ephesians 1:16-17).

But you have an anointing from the Holy One, and you know all things (1John 2:20).

But the anointing which you have received from Him abides in you, and you do not need that anyone teach you; but as the same anointing teaches you concerning all things, and that anointing is true, and is not a lie, and just as it has taught you, you will abide in Him (1John 2:27)

10. **Seven-fold Anointing of Daniel**

There is a man in your kingdom in whom is the Spirit of the Holy God. And in the days of your father, light and understanding and wisdom, like the wisdom of the gods, were found in him; and King Nebuchadnezzar your father—your father the king—made him chief of the magicians, astrologers, Chaldeans, and soothsayers.

Inasmuch as an excellent spirit, knowledge, understanding, interpreting dreams, solving riddles, and explaining enigmas were found in this Daniel, whom the king named Belteshazzar, now let Daniel be called, and he will show the interpretation (Daniel 5:11-12).

11. **Manifold Wisdom of God**

and to make all see what is the fellowship of the mystery, which from the beginning of the ages has been hidden in God who created all things through Jesus Christ;

to the intent that now the manifold wisdom of God might be made known by the church to the principalities and powers in the heavenly places, according to the eternal purpose which He accomplished in Christ Jesus our Lord,

in whom we have boldness and access with confidence through faith in Him (Ephesians 3:9-12).

12. **Angelic assistance**

For He shall give His angels charge over you, to keep you in all your ways (Psalm 91:11).

And of the angels He says: "Who makes His angels spirits And His ministers a flame of fire" (Hebrews 1:7).

Are they not all ministering spirits sent forth to minister for them who shall be heirs of salvation? (Hebrews 1:14).

13. **Seven Spirits of God**

The Spirit of the LORD shall rest upon Him, the Spirit of wisdom and understanding, the Spirit of counsel and might, the Spirit of knowledge and of the fear of the LORD (Isaiah 11:2).

And I looked, and behold, in the midst of the throne and of the four living creatures, and in the midst of the elders, stood a Lamb as though it had been slain, having seven horns and seven eyes, which are the seven Spirits of God sent out into all the earth (Revelation 5:6).

14. **Gifts of the Spirit**

There are diversities of gifts, but the same Spirit.

There are differences of ministries, but the same Lord.

And there are diversities of activities, but it is the same God who works all in all. But the manifestation of the Spirit is given to each one for the profit of all:

for to one is given the word of wisdom through the Spirit, to another the word of knowledge through the same Spirit,

to another faith by the same Spirit, to another gifts of healings by the same Spirit,

to another the working of miracles, to another prophecy, to another discerning of spirits, to another different kinds of tongues, to another the interpretation of tongues (1Corinthians 12:4-10).

15. **Biblical meditation**

Be angry, and do not sin. Meditate within your heart on your bed, and be still (Psalm 4:4).

This Book of the Law shall not depart from your mouth, but you shall meditate in it day and night, that you may observe to do according to all that is written in it. For then you will make your way prosperous, and then you will have good success (Joshua 1:8).

16. **Favor of God**

For You, O LORD, will bless the righteous; with favor You will surround him as with a shield (Psalm 5:12).

17. **The anointing of recognition**

And the evil spirit answered and said, "Jesus I know, and Paul I know; but who are you?" (Acts 19:15).

Knowing, therefore, the terror of the Lord, we persuade men; but we are well known to God, and I also trust are well known in your consciences (Galatians 4:9).

But now after you have known God, or rather are known by God (2Corinthians 5:11).

18. **Ministering unto the Lord**

As they ministered to the Lord and fasted, the Holy Spirit said.... (Acts 13:2).

19. **Peace**

Peace I leave with you, My peace I give to you; not as the world gives do I give to you. Let not your heart be troubled, neither let it be afraid (John 14:27).

And let the peace of God rule in your hearts, to which also you were called in one body; and be thankful (Colossians 3:15).

20. **Word of your testimony**

And they overcame him by the blood of the Lamb and by the word of their testimony, and they did not love their lives to the death (Revelation 12:11).

We must know our measure of rule to be effective in advancing His kingdom (2Corinthians 10:12-16).

The Emerging Daniel Company must model humility and prayer as the Prophet Daniel did. These two things attract the presence of His Spirit. Having broken and contrite hearts for those in authority with a biblical worldview will also cause the Lord to promote us with kingdom authority. We are given the mandate to overcome. To overcome means to conquer or to gain victory over something. It is said that the inherent thought in the word *overcome* is to be a conqueror or victorious in a contest or conflict. We know that because of Christ living inside of us, we can actually be overcomers (Romans 8:37). Being overcomers in this transitional generation means that we hold fast until the seventh angel sounds and the loud voices in heaven say, *"The kingdoms of this world have become the kingdoms of our*

Lord and of His Christ, and He shall reign forever and ever" (Revelation 11:15).

WHO ARE THE OVERCOMERS?

Randy DeMain writes in his book, *Dominion Surges,* "the promises and prophecies of Christ will be fully experienced by a generation of overcomers, a generation who will come out and be separate, who will wash their robes in righteousness. These overcoming saints are positioning themselves to live and minister out of the presence of the Lord. They are that greatly desired church Jesus is building; the church the gates of Hades will not prevail against. This church is a militant group of believers who are filled with a sense of timing and purpose. They refuse to be denied and are determined to see His purposes fulfilled in the days ahead. The apostolic generation that is coming forth is not satisfied with the incomplete conquest experienced by those who have come before them. While we have learned great lessons from them and have benefited greatly from their faith and sacrifice, much is yet to be overcome."

The invitation and call to overcome is given to all believers. However, not all choose to become the overcomers who are given positions of authority in His coming kingdom (Revelation 3:21). What are we to overcome? The world, the flesh, and the enemy. To overcome denotes inheriting the kingdom. As sons and daughters of God, we have inheritances available to us. The first is called a *sonship inheritance,* which belongs to every believer. The other is an inheritance from the Lord and is conditional. This inheritance is earned by the lifestyle of choices, faithfulness, and obedience to the Lord. The overcomers will rule and reign with Him because of their life of devotion to the Lord.

To overcome means to gain the victory over something (the world, the flesh, or the devil). Overcomers are victorious in the conflict that was set before them—they are those who allow the true Overcomer (Jesus) to live His life through them (Romans 8:37). Chuck and Nancy Missler write: "Overcomers are those Christians who by being partakers of Christ's eternal life are able to conquer, prevail, and subdue the temptations of the world, the desires of the flesh, and the wiles of the devil. They have learned to love with God's love, make faith choices according to His wisdom, and depend upon His power to accomplish their deeds" (*Kingdom Power and Glory*).

Because we are in turbulent times, we need more messages concerning overcoming, inheriting the kingdom, and occupying until He comes. Study what was promised to the overcomers in the seven churches in the Book of Revelation. Equipping centers, schools of ministry that have an open heaven over them, and a quickening spirit must prepare a generation to be overcomers. Overcoming implies maturity and transformation into "Christ-likeness." Just growing in spiritual gifts can still produce immature and unproductive believers.

Here are some characteristic of overcomers:

1. They remain loyal to God (Revelation 2:1–3)
2. They do not deny Christ (Revelation 3:8)
3. They do not defile their garments (Revelation 3:4)
4. They are faithful in tribulation (Revelation 2:8, 10).
5. They keep His Word or the word of His patience (Revelation 3:10)

If we want to inherit the Kingdom, we must be overcomers. It is God's will for all of us to overcome.

How do the Scriptures say we can overcome? By believing and exercising our faith in the authority and power of God. On page 226 in *Kingdom Power and Glory*, it states, "The Word of God is what gives us this authority and the Spirit of God is what gives us power. These two phenomenal gifts (the authority and power of Christ) are not only keys to overcoming the world, the flesh, and the devil (all the challenges in this life) but they are also keys to the future millennial kingdom. Again, knowing His presence and knowing how to apply the Word are our keys. Putting on the whole armor of God, which is being properly dressed, is a must. No soldier in their right mind would not be prepared, trained, and dressed for war."

The message of the overcomer is that the enemy has no ability to defeat Christ, the One who leads us to victory. An overcoming generation is a breakthrough generation that will not be contained. *"The one who breaks open will come up before them; they will break out, pass through the gate and go out by it; their king will pass before them, with the Lord at their head"* (Micah 2:13). As overcomers we will receive the fullness of Him and the fullness of our inheritance in Him.

It is time to train, equip, and impart the zeal of the Lord of Hosts to this transitional generation. Growing in His love and kingdom authority in this season are prerequisites for obtaining our inheritance and occupying places of influence for the purpose of advancing the kingdom.

CHAPTER SIX

EMERGING NEW LEADERSHIP

"*To everything there is a season, a time for every purpose under heaven*" (Ecclesiastes 3:1*)*. In this season of the Spirit, I see new leaders emerging who have been being prepared for what is upon us and that which is unfolding. To emerge is defined as: to rise, come forth or come out into view. Some, like Samuel, will arise from the place of having ministered unto the Lord, experiencing His manifest Presence. As priests, their function is to intercede for the Lord's people and give instruction in the ways of righteousness; calling the people to be set apart and consecrated for His purposes. Samuel was a transitional leader in a transitional time. Like Samuel, this leadership will be transitional, arising in a transitional time.

Also emerging are the Joshuas coming forth after being mentored, matured, and commissioned. He was brought forth to help a generation enter into their inheritance. Joshua was full of the Spirit of Wisdom, which he received through an impartation from Moses (Deuteronomy 34:9). He was instructed by Moses and mentored by him, as he watched the Lord working through him and the faithfulness of living a life of obedience. The Joshuas are given the charge of causing the people to inherit (Deuteronomy 3:28).

Accessing the promise in I Peter 1:3–5 is part of the commissioning for this generation—receiving an inheritance that has been reserved in heaven and now ready to be revealed in the last times (vs. 5). This leadership encounters the Lord to receive their instructions (Joshua 5:13–15). Being instructed to be strong and very courageous, they are coming forth to see the Lord of Hosts dispossess the giants in the land.

Now is the time for the Daniels who are set to come out into view. They are those who pray for government leaders, nations and global gates. Recently, I had lunch with Ian Cole, an interesting guy who loves the Lord. Ian had just come from New York City where he and several others were praying for the United Nations. Meeting briefly, I shared what was on my heart. Upon hearing that the name of our ministry is The Emerging Daniel Company, Ian exclaimed that the last time they (a group of prayer leaders from around the world) prayed, the Lord asked, "When are you going to release the Daniels?"

Remember, to emerge means: to rise (Samuels), to come forth (the Joshuas), and to come out into view (the Daniels).

I see apostolic and prophetic teams coming into divine alliance. All leadership will need mature seers and watchers around them in this transitional season. The ministry function is to see. Daniel was a seer of visions. King David had a seer named Gad and another named Heman. Gad was the king's seer in the word of God, and Heman saw the songs of God (1Chronicles 25:5). Seers are at their best when they are in relationship with leadership. The leadership chooses the seer; the seer does not choose the leadership. The relationship must grow to where they learn spiritual protocol. In other words, they must know their boundaries (EDC recommends our good friend Jim Driscoll's book, *The Modern Seer: A Biblical Gift in Today's Context*). We are called to watch the Lord Himself admonish us concerning watching. To watch is to be awake and alert in our spirits.

> *But of that day and hour no one knows, not even the angels in heaven nor the Son, but only the Father.*
>
> *Take heed, watch and pray; for you do not know when the time is.*
>
> *It is like a man going to a far country, who left his house and gave authority to his servants, and to each his work, and commanded the doorkeeper to watch.*
>
> *Watch therefore, for you do not know when the master of the house is coming—in evening, at midnight, at the crowing of the rooster, or in the morning* (Mark 13:32-35).

The watchmen anointing operates to see the things in the Spirit as well as what the enemy is up to. Watching is the way we receive the preparation, strength, and supernatural courage that will be needed in this transitional season. Watching is a lifestyle of encountering the Lord; watching prevents the realm of darkness from stealing or destroying our inheritance. Watchers are now on the lookout for our time of visitation (Luke 19:44).

Because we are in a season of acceleration, both light and darkness are intensifying in the authority needed for this hour. We must apprehend. Without the Lord's help, we will not make it. Nothing will work in this season except knowing the King and advancing His kingdom.

The purifying process of the Lord has been at work (2Peter 1:5–11). The Lord is seeking and searching for a mature and trustworthy leadership who stays in their God-appointed assignment and measure of rule (2Corinthians 10:12–18).

Abiding in our call and flowing with the Spirit empowers us to understand the times and season. Calling on the wisdom that comes from above (James 3:17–18) will empower us to steward who and what He has entrusted to us.

Because we are emerging out of the old and into the new, we will need to learn how to follow the Lord with passion, focus, and discipline in the unchartered waters. A leadership joined to the Head, in intimacy, will keep us from drowning. Leadership summits are a must for these times, preparing kingdom leaders who will affect the seven spheres of society.

The releasing and maturation of the apostolic and prophetic grace to establish His government is being dispatched. Cities, regions, and national leaders must work together to become the one voice that changes atmospheres. Preparing for the outpouring (Acts 2, Joel 2), and the glory (Numbers 14:21) is our ultimate assignment as well as being lights as in Daniel 12:3, shining and leading.

With all that is occurring in these turbulent and glorious times, one thing we must do can be found in Hebrews 10:35, *"Therefore do not cast away your confidence, which has great reward."* As we wait for the next step, we cannot cast away our confidence.

We are at an intersection in time, during which we will see the demonstration of the Spirit, favor, wealth transference, and houses of prayer being established. In the midst of the turbulence, the Lord is providing for every area of our lives. We can pray as they prayed in Acts 4:29–30, for all boldness and that we will see signs and wonders. As leaders, we are called "harvesters of the harvest." The Emerging Daniel Company is developing equipping centers connected to local churches that are positioning themselves to receive all that the Lord has promised. We all need to grow in spiritual sensitivity and sensitivity to the Holy Spirit.

One of the Emerging Daniel Company's mandates is to prepare, equip, strengthen leadership, and reclaim mantles of revelation and power for the purpose of advancing His kingdom. However, we cannot advance without a fight. The fight is on! All battles are first won in the Spirit—then in the natural.

We are in a war. We must help God's people know how to dress for the battle and prepare them to stand (Ephesians 6:10–18). In all that is happening, whether good, bad, or ugly, we must stay humble, and walk in humility with a broken and contrite spirit.

Humility is a key that helps accelerate the revelation needed for the next step. Understanding spiritual warfare is absolutely essential for this emerging leadership. This should already have been learned, but let me say it again. "Learning how to behave in the cave will prevent needless casualties of war." Let us master the place of worship and communion first. Abiding in the secret place is where His strategies, war counsel, and insights come from. These things also come from the Lord of Hosts Who is wonderful in counsel and excellent in guidance.

This new emerging leadership will be empowered and taught by the seven Spirits of God (Isaiah 11:2). In order for us to fulfill the greater works that were prophesied by Jesus, we are going to need these seven impartations from the Spirit of the Lord. It is a complete representation of His revelation which is the seven eyes and seven horns of power (Revelation 5:6). Daniel is our prototype who demonstrated a mature life in God and the essence of the anointing for his sphere of influence. We must pray, fast, and seek the Lord for the release of these mantles today. Only those who have integrity, character, maturity, and purity of heart will be endowed with them. Walking in these mantles gives us authority with God and with men.

Manifestations of the Spirit of the Lord

1. **The Spirit of the Lord**
   He teaches us how to experience the reality of the kingdom of heaven along with authority, power, and dominion. He also teaches us about sonship and rulership, and how to bring the government and divine order of God into the earth. We are taught about the glory realm.

2. **The Spirit of Wisdom**
   The Spirit of Wisdom is the supernatural ability of God that comes upon our spirits to see Jesus as He is and receive a spiritual understanding and knowledge of God's Word that enables us to know what to do, when to do it, and how to do it in every situation. It also reveals God's manifold and unsearchable wisdom and secrets affecting His plans and purposes. It means a deeper intimacy into the things of God.

3. **The Spirit of Understanding**
   The Spirit of Understanding or revelation is a comprehension of the things of God providing understanding with the mind giving insight with perception. Wisdom and understanding means the insight into the true nature of things with the ability to discern mode of action with a view to their results. It is the ability to not only know the things of God, but also the application of them practically. Revelation is the comprehension imparted into our spirits from the Holy Spirit and transmitted into our minds. It is the voice of God speaking to our spirits and informing our minds that which God is going to do, the unfolding of hidden secrets to us by the Holy Spirit, and the revealing of mysteries and insight into the future.

4. The Spirit of Counsel

The Spirit of Counsel is advice, plans, or admonitions of prudence to provide leadership and proper decision making to achieve God's plan and purpose. The Hebrew word for counsel used numerous times in the Old Testament is *etsah* and is translated as counsel, advice, advisement, or purpose. One of the first occurrences is in Exodus 18:9, when Jethro gives counsel to Moses concerning the leadership of Israel. The Spirit of counsel grants advice from God's throne and provides the perfect plan or strategy to achieve a specific mandate. The Lord is the Spirit of Counsel (Isaiah 9:6). In Isaiah 28:29, it says that this also comes from the Lord of hosts, Who is wonderful in counsel and excellent in guidance.

5. The Spirit of Might

Might is taken from the Hebrew word *gebuwrah* and is defined as power, strength, or force producing valor, victory, and mighty deeds. The Spirit of Might illustrates and demonstrates the marvelous acts and miraculous powers of the Holy Spirit (Deuteronomy 3:24). Responding to His counsel releases might.

6 The Spirit of Knowledge

The Spirit of Knowledge is taken from the Hebrew word *da'ath* and could be defined as spiritually imparted knowledge, skill, awareness, comprehension, and discernment that are conveyed as instruction and insight from God's heart and sovereignty. Da'ath also denotes intimate relational *knowing*. It is the same word used in Genesis when scripture says, "Adam knew his wife."

7. The Spirit of (reverential) Fear of the Lord

The Spirit of reverential Fear of the Lord is taken from the Hebrew word *yir'ah* meaning awe, inspiring, terrible, and awesome. Reverential fear in its purest form is birthed out of love. We fear God because we love Him and have a revelatory knowledge of His nature and character. It is a work of the Holy Spirit that produces this reverential awe of God. The fear of the Lord does not make us afraid of God, but instead catapults our faith into the supernatural realm through a revelation of how great He truly is.

Revelation 1:4 says, *"Grace to you and peace from Him who is and who was and who is to come and from the seven Spirits who are before His throne")*.

The new leadership will come from every tribe, tongue, people, and nation, as kings and priests to our God who shall reign on the earth.

As leaders, we must declare and teach that we are destined to reign on the earth. We are called as saints to ultimately possess the kingdom, not to just hold down the fort until He comes. Daniel 7:21-22 says: *"I was watching; and the same horn was making war against the saints, and prevailing against them until the Ancient of Days came, and a judgment was made in favor of the saints of the Most High, and the time came for the saints to possess the kingdom."*

The government of God that is being established on the earth is being unfolded by the fivefold ministries mentioned in Ephesians 4. *"And He Himself gave some to be apostles, some prophets, some evangelists, and some pastors and teachers, for the equipping of the saints for the work of ministry, for the edifying of the body of Christ, till we all come to the unity of the faith and of the knowledge of the Son of God, to a mature man, to the measure of the stature of the fullness of Christ"* (Ephesians 4:11-13).

Every leadership team must seek the Lord on how this is to be administrated in their local assembly. One thing is very certain and that is every believer must come to the unity of the faith and the full stature of Christ. From the beginning, God established two foundational legs for the body — apostolic teams and elders. The two forms of leadership were local — the presbyters (called a group of elders) and mobile leadership (called apostolic teams). Both of these are foundational in the New Testament, and are dependent upon the grace of God and the guidance of the Holy Spirit for direction and insight. The apostolic was for the expansion and advancement into different spheres for the kingdom. They have the "go therefore" ministry (Matthew 28:18-19). They are the sent ones who have a heart for regions (2Corinthians 10:13-16).

Derek Prince writes in his book, *Rediscovering God's Church:* "Notice that the word sphere occurs five times and the word regions once in 2Corinthians 10:13-16. How perfectly this fits the mind of the apostle! First he has a sense of his sphere; the geographic and spiritual limitations of his authority. The essence of this ministry is to be moving out. Presently we are in the infant stage of the restoration of the apostolic. Those called to this ministry are in and have been in the refiner's fire to purify their motives and to develop endurance and perseverance. There will be an emerging apostolic ministry that is real and pure and true. We are experiencing a lot of the false and the immature professing to be apostles. Title flashing is now common in the body of Christ. However, this does not negate the fact that the Lord will raise up a true and mature apostolic ministry—the Lord will produce the real. The Spirit of the Lord will restore it to biblical stature."

Derek Prince gives seven key marks of a true apostle:

1. A heart for regions beyond
2. The ability to fulfill all the special tasks of an apostle (master builder)
3. The establishment of churches that reflect the apostle's heart
4. A desire for team ministry
5. Accountability toward the sending church
6. Signs and wonders
7. Perseverance

The building of apostolic teams should be done by those who have a fatherly anointing. The team is to be formed and developed by selection that comes from prayer and seeking the counsel of the Lord. Team members must be team players, and joined to the leader. The team should be made up of prophets/seers, evangelists, pastors and teachers. They must walk in the light with one another and model the biblical characteristics of body life.

In the book, *Apostles Today*, by Barney Coombs, he gives the ten Golden Rules of body life.

1. They should be devoted to one another in brotherly love (Romans 12:10)
2. Each one should regard the others as more important than himself (Philippians 2:3).
3. They should give preference to one another (Romans 12:10).
4. They should, through love, serve one another (Galatians 5:13).
5. They should be joyous and carry a positive demeanor (1Thessalonians 5:6).
6. They should encourage and spur one another on (Hebrews (10:24- 25).

7. They should walk in forgiveness (Colossians 3:13).
8. They should do all things without grumbling (Philippians 2:14).
9. They should strive to maintain the unity of the Spirit (2Timothy 2:24).
10. They should confess their faults to one another (James 5:16).

A healthy apostolic ministry will equip and reproduce healthy and mature saints. The two main functions of the apostle are to establish properly ordered churches and ministries and to bring order to those that already exist (Titus 1:5).

Concerning the other four ministries, much has been written already, especially about the prophet and the prophetic ministry. There is a difference between immature prophetic gifting and false prophets. We are experiencing a measure of inconsistency among those we respect in the office of a prophet. To this day, we have major international prophets saying different things concerning the destiny and what God is doing with President Barack Obama. If there is contradiction on that level, how do we expect to be the voices to the nations? There is much growth needed in this hour and the Lord is well able to accomplish it.

The five-fold ministry is the spiritual government being established for the perfecting of the saints. The saints are to grow up into their purpose and fulfill the Lord's destiny for their lives.

UNITY OF THE FAITH

Emerging leaders, through their understanding of Scripture and insight into revelation, need to develop an unshakeable faith in God. This does not mean they eventually reach a place where their faith is so huge that their life becomes simple and easy. However, it *does* mean they understand what Peter said: *"Blessed be the God and Father of our Lord Jesus Christ who according to His abundant mercy has begotten us again to a living hope through the resurrection of Jesus Christ from the dead, to an inheritance incorruptible and undefiled and that does not fade away, reserved in heaven for you who are kept by the power of God through faith for salvation ready to be revealed in the last time"* (1 Peter 1:3-5). Confess the Word—speak and call to remembrance the promises God has given you and believe in your heart. This is faith. Applying faith moves us into the realm of the Spirit.

When we put our faith in Him, we believe for one or more of the following:

- His wisdom to guide us
- His plan to be executed effectively
- His favor on our life
- A miracle from His hand
- For our strength to endure until He acts

My friend Paul Keith Davis writes in an article, *Our Need for True Leadership:*

> *There is a present need for clarity and honorable leadership to emerge with a credible prophetic voice to provide direction and divine wisdom. With an increasing emphasis on the emergence of God's divine government; there is an equal demand for biblical understanding of God's promises for the end-of-the age generation. There are clear spiritual endowments being imparted to those groomed and prepared for governmental responsibility. Never before has there been a greater need for the spirits of wisdom and revelation promised in Ephesians 1:17-19 saying:*

That the God of our Lord Jesus Christ, the Father of glory, may give to you a spirit of wisdom and of revelation in the knowledge of Him. I pray that the eyes of your heart may be enlightened, so that you will know what is the hope of His calling, what are the riches of the glory of His inheritance in the saints, and what is the surpassing greatness of His power toward us who believe.

Like Daniel and his three friends in Babylonian captivity, we desperately need the impartation of heavenly wisdom and knowledge as well as intelligence in all manner of writing and literature. We desperately need insight and interpretation of our dreams and visions (Daniel 1:17).

It is my perspective that all true spiritual leadership is birthed out of friendship with the Lord. He once told His disciples that He no longer considered them servants, but friends. From that place of intimacy, God's mysteries, secrets and strategies are imparted that convey the Father's thoughts and aspirations for this generation.

God's governmental model empowers people to realize their fullest potential. Empowerment comes through our lives as we submit to the Lordship of Jesus and become spiritually aligned with those He has set and placed in His government within His kingdom.

CHAPTER SEVEN

PLACES OF ENCOUNTER

It has now been about seven years since I received this revelation concerning the Lord's plan to establish places where His people encounter His presence and glory. At that time, the Lord started talking to me about creative worship art centers. I was reminded about a word given to me about developing a culture for these creative prophetic people. We are now in a season where houses of prayer are being established all over the world (Tabernacle of David).

Historically, the Lord has raised up reformers to restore Davidic worship. Restoration and reformation are throne room initiatives being released for the purpose of His presence and glory to fill the earth. *"Prepare the way of the Lord; make straight in the desert a highway for our God. Every valley shall be exalted and every mountain and hill brought low; the crooked places shall be made straight and the rough places smooth* (into places of encounter); *the glory of the Lord shall be revealed, and all flesh shall see it together; for the mouth of the Lord has spoken* (Isaiah 40:3-5). Scriptures reveal that there have been times when the Lord restored worship and praise unto Him in the hearts of the people, then in places where the corporate community creates an atmosphere to encounter Him. Kings and priests restored temple worship like King Hezekiah, Ezra, Nehemiah, and so on.

The 21st century expression of the tabernacle includes strategies, downloads, and witty inventions. We need to cultivate a passion for His presence. It will enthrone God in our lives and situations; it will enlarge Him in our hearts and minds; it will enlist God to move on our behalf; it will bring Him enjoyment, which is the primary reason to worship Him. Soaking in His presence like Samuel will teach us how to rest in Him (1Samuel 3:1-6). As we seek Him, we will find Him (Matthew 7:7).

CORPORATELY ENTERING THROUGH THE DOOR OF REVELATION AND MYSTERY

Divine inspiration is being released. In this new season, we have access to His manifested presence. The glory of God is the manifested presence and person of the Lord Jesus Christ. Because the glory of the latter house will be greater than the former (Haggai 2:9), we will need to learn how to corporately cultivate atmospheres. Those with the priestly/kingly anointing will need to be instructed by the Spirit of grace on how to administrate with spiritual sensitivity His presence. This is where those who are trained in the order of Melchizedek come in. We will be taught His ways. Our major focus will be on His presence and being carriers of the glory.

Our total fulfillment will be a direct result of our communion with Him. One of the outcomes of communion is creativity, and creativity releases new things and new potential. The first attribute we see of God is Creator. We are at the place in time where a whole new wave of spiritual creativity is needed. One of The Emerging Daniel Company events is "Axis of Spiritual Creativity" with the purpose in mind to capture and ignite the unbridled spirit of creativity in each person present through spontaneous worship, expressions of praise and adoration, teachings with practical instructions, and impartation. As we minister unto the Lord and stand in His Presence, we receive life, light, and renewed vision.

These places of encounter will be conducive to bringing the pieces together, in order that we may move together as a unified corporate body.

THE SECRET PLACE

Pleasing God and knowing that we were created for His pleasure must become a reality that moves from the head to the heart.

Jesus restored eternal life (John 6:53–58). In doing so, He restored the way to intimacy. Before the Word became flesh, we see the result of intimacy with Him foreshadowed through the lives of Enoch and Elijah. The first law of the Spirit—*"all things consist and have their being in Him"* (Acts 17:28; Romans 11:36).

Ministering unto the Lord should be our highest priority. Passionately pursuing the secret place of the Most High "in season" is absolutely non-negotiable. On a daily basis we must drink from the well of His Presence. Living waters quench the thirst of the desperate and revive the spirit of the weary. This well is where the place of revelation flows freely. Choosing intimacy with Him is choosing life. It is the life of God that gives us light (John 1:4).

In His presence, the living Word is manifested (Hebrew 4:12–13). We receive truth in His presence. All of the things we are growing *in* and giving language to, must come from a place of encounter with Him. Apostolic teams, marketplace ministry, seers, intercessors and the fivefold ministry must all emerge from the well of His presence. Corporate ministry to the affections of the Lord is a strategy that will bring immediate results. The Spirit of unity in the bond of peace will help us not to be deceived nor shipwrecked in our faith during these transitional times.

There is much said about the sons of Zadok who, because of faithfulness and loyalty during times of apostasy, were rewarded a place of honor (Ezekiel 44:15-16). However, it was Zadok who set the example his sons could follow (1Chronicles 16:37-39).

Preparing to enter His presence or learning to wait by the well of His presence means waiting, watching and listening. We need to do a lot of reflective observation and journaling of our life experiences so the anointing can be transferred.

THE SCROLL OF REVELATION

In Ezekiel 3:1-4, the eating of the scroll of revelation caused the Word to proceed out of Ezekiel's mouth. The Lord is releasing instruction both to the body of Christ and to the angelic realm concerning cities, regions, and nations. The strategies of heaven are being released and received by a company of forerunners who are commissioned to declare His Word and demonstrate the Kingdom. I believe the war room in heaven is stirred with much activity and excitement. This is the season for the Lord to receive a measure of the reward for His suffering. As joint heirs of Christ, the saints are being positioned to receive recompense, restitution, reimbursement, *and* restoration. Experiencing the economy of the kingdom is the next throne room initiative we need to learn to walk in. The reality of the kingdom on earth as it is in heaven must be demonstrated in this season. Being seated in heavenly places and operating from this position must become a lifestyle, not just a doctrine. Heavenly places are seats of dominion where the activities of the heavens take place on earth. Some heavenly places stated in the Bible are in the heavenly places in Christ Jesus. However, there is a similar structure imitated by Satan as stated in Ephesians 6:12: *"for we do not wrestle against flesh and blood but against principalities, against powers, against the rulers of the darkness of this age, against spiritual hosts of wicked-ness in the heavenly places."*

KEYS TO HEAVEN'S ECONOMY

Our friend, Shawn Bolz, had an encounter with an angel some years ago. In his book, *Keys to Heaven's Economy,* the revelation given to him concerning the economy of Heaven is more relevant now than when he first received this insight. Let us release our faith to access what's available to us as was shown to Shawn by the Minister of Finance.

PLACES OF PROVISION

The LORD will send a blessing on your barns and on everything you put your hand to. The LORD your God will bless you in the land He is giving you (Deuteronomy 28:8).

In 1997, he had a supernatural experience that dramatically marked his life. He was transported to a heavenly realm and taken to a huge warehouse. It was so vast that he explains he could not find the room's perimeters—he could not distinguish the ceiling or walls—even though the room was enclosed. He says it reminded him of how much space there is in the eternal heart of God. An angel who oversaw the storehouse was assigned to show him around. As he took Shawn on a tour through different sections of the building, he was gripped by anticipation. "What is this place?" he asked. The angel's eyes lit up. He smiled and replied, "This is the storehouse of heaven. Every provision that will ever be needed in this age for Jesus to receive the fullness of His inheritance is here, ready and waiting for those who would partner with Him and would call it forth."

The revelation of this abundant and pre-planned provision was too much for Shawn to comprehend. Not only did God the Father know us before we were even in our mothers' wombs, but He designed a comprehensive plan of provision that would last until His Son returns. Being transfixed by the awe of God, by how He literally has created provision for us that is so real, all we need to do is access it. No wonder Jesus taught us to ask the Father to manifest everything we need on earth as it is in heaven! It really exists there now!

The angel took Shawn through heaven's storehouse for a long time, looking at the many types of provisions. We mention a few of the areas shown to Shawn just to build your perspective of what is available to us. I hope as you read this that God begins to instill a desire within your heart to survey the storehouse for yourself.

THE DEPARTMENT OF CREATIVE MIRACLES

As Shawn describes what he saw as he continued to travel with the angel as they walked down aisles of glory, it was unlike any place he had ever been. Eventually, they reached a room within the larger warehouse wherein the aisles in this room were so large that Shawn was unable to describe all that he saw. But he shares that in this warehouse were aisles upon aisles of body parts with names and dates of those who would eventually receive them. Can you imagine that God has already made provision for various limbs and all we need is the faith to manifest it?

When Shawn asked his angelic companion, "What is this room?" he said he felt like weeping. The angel replied, "This is the Department of Creative Miracles."

HEAVENLY MANNA

In another section Shawn noticed angels preparing food. Every type of meat healthful for human consumption filled the table. A vast quantity of breads, oats, milk, clean water, and vegetables had been accumulated. A grand preparation was going on, and Shawn says he immediately thought of the wedding supper of the Lamb in Revelation 19:9.

"I know what you are thinking, but the foods here are not for His banquet," the angel said. "These foods will be called forth and given through miraculous provision and multiplication for the poor of the earth and the poor in spirit."

A SUPERNATURAL FAITH DIMENSION

Next Shawn describes walking toward a cloud of color and light that resembled pictures captured by the Hubble Telescope, and when he entered the cloud, he found himself in the middle of magnificent light. Other people were in the cloud; they seemed to be praying on earth, somehow accessing this place in God's heart. As they prayed in agreement with what was available in Heaven, the limited natural realm expanded to admit the miraculous power of God.

Then as quickly as he had entered this cloud, he was back in the storehouse on the other side.

Shawn noticed that his angelic companion had not traveled into the cloud with him. "That is a place in the Father's heart reserved for humans," he explained. I realized that God had designed us to commune with His heart in a way that even angels could not.

ROOMS OF DIVINE ARCHITECTURE

Next, Shawn describes a different area in the storehouse. "Welcome to the rooms of Divine Architecture," announced my angelic companion.

Miniature models of buildings were everywhere. There were materials that were fully prepared for architectural works and new types of structures and buildings that had been assembled to withstand global calamities.

There were entire city blocks living and breathing with people and traffic flowing through them based on new demographic plans from heaven; they seemed to already exist in finished forms. God's plans are this complete, needing only our agreement in order to manifest in our generation.

Circular tables were overlaid with plans and blueprints for various kinds of buildings that would be built to glorify God: stadiums, places of worship, businesses, schools, and hospitals.

Each plan had a seal on it. Some of the seals had names and dates; others just had names, while some were left unmarked, waiting for whoever would commit to that plan to bring forth the name as well as the purpose of Jesus. What an opportunity and occupation to be an architect with access to Heaven's divine architecture!

THE CREATIVE INVENTIONS SECTION

After this, they were quickly carried away by the Spirit to a different section called Creative Inventions. Lights and colors swirled around, and the Holy Spirit seemed to hover and flash like lightning.

Every type of technology was represented here: agricultural, computer science, medical. Many cures for diseases were in this section. Toys were here, sound devices, video and multimedia machines—so many basic materials already known to humanity that could be combined in new configurations to create revolutionary advancements for the earth. The Spirit of Revelation would have to reveal the various combinations.

The same creative Spirit inventing science was also inventing the arts. In the same section, were many rooms that were specifically dedicated to the creative arts. Because there is coming such an astounding release of heaven's arts upon the earth, creative arts centers will pop up in cities around the world, redefining the boundaries between the different artistic media and their expression and housing many artistic forms of expression in a single building.

HEAVEN'S MUSIC STOREROOM

At the edge of the creative arts section was a fourth section—Heaven's Music Storeroom. It was in full use.

The music arts section was especially interesting because it overlapped the very throne room of heaven. So many instruments were being played and so many songs were being sung. Sounds that had not yet been created, accompanied by modified and even brand-new instruments, were rampant. Songbooks full of new expressions had been written to unlock hearts and woo them to a deeper intimacy with God. The number of songbooks seemed infinite, and all of them pleased God immensely—the only One who would ever be able to count the reams upon reams of songs still to be written for Him. King Solomon had touched this creative realm; he is reputed to have written more than a thousand songs in his lifetime that glorified God. Imagine when an entire generation taps into this celestial sphere!

A PICTURE OF HEAVEN'S ECONOMY

After reading what the Angel of Finance showed to Shawn in this experience, we can see the key to this economy: Faith, which is living life outside of the box, prophetic declarations, and proclamations and contending for our inheritance with the wisdom of God and the anointing of the sons of Issachar. Where does it all begin? By cultivating the secret place and pursing passionately His presence.

The economy of heaven and the transference of wealth (Proverbs 13:22) are for the purpose of advancing His kingdom agenda. A new mindset that recognizes and seizes opportunities for redemptive purposes will be needed in this season.

Let us learn to wait and learn of Him. We can only mobilize the work after being in His Presence. Divine guidance is the intelligence we need to navigate through these turbulent times. Supernatural knowing, insights, strategies and understanding spring forth from dwelling in the secret place (Psalm 91:1). Loving Him, knowing Him, and understanding and cooperating with what He is doing is the order of our times.

PROPHETIC WORSHIP THROUGH THE ARTS

As a part of the Emerging Daniel Company, the goal of everything we do is invite His presence. It's that simple. In everything we do, we are trying to catch His eye. The worshipping church has received a charge from the throne room of heaven: Pursue excellence in the arts for the purpose of proclaiming and revealing the glory of God in the earth.

> *Let them praise His name in chorus and choir and with the [single or group] dance; let them sing praises to Him with the tambourine and lyre!*
> *For the Lord takes pleasure in His people; He will beautify the humble with salvation and adorn the wretched with victory.*
> *Let the saints be joyful in the glory and beauty [which God confers upon them]; let them sing for joy upon their beds* (Psalm 149:3–5, Amplified).

PLACES OF HIS PRESENCE

In Acts 15:5–19, a council made up of apostles and elders gathered together to consider the demands of a sect of the Pharisees who were requiring newly converted Gentiles to keep the law and become circumcised. Peter, Barnabas, and Paul testified to the mighty works of God among the Gentiles. James confirmed that the words of the prophets agreed with what was taking place and that the revelation of the rebuilding of the Tabernacle of David was connected to the finished works of Christ (Amos 9:11).

All of the New Testament apostles recognized and agreed with the conclusion. So it stands to spiritual reason that the apostolic is assigned to rebuild and set up Tabernacle of David houses of prayer for all nations, in all cities and geographic regions.

Tabernacles of David are established so that God's manifested presence can be experienced by all. In America alone, there are 101 people groups who need to encounter the well of His Presence and obtain their spiritual inheritance (Deuteronomy 32:8).

Some of the principles and insights about rebuilding the Tabernacle of David were shared in an interview with Bob and Diane Hartman, a couple that has studied and prayed for the restoration of the Tabernacle of David since the late 1970s. They were involved in the Charismatic Movement in the late 60s and 70s. Accustomed to the sounds of praise and worship, they found themselves wanting something more, but had no idea where to find what they were looking for. The following are excerpts from that interview:

A friend invited us to attend something she called a symposium. Not knowing what a symposium was, but knowing this friend shared the same hunger for God, we went with her. The word "symposium" originally meant a drinking party (the Greek verb "sympotein" means to drink together). In Western culture, the word has evolved to mean a meeting or conference for the public discussion or embracing of some topic, especially one in which the participants make presentations or actually participate as the gathering progresses and unfolds. In this case, it was like a living and powerful demonstration of the principles this group came together to impart and release. When we walked into the symposium, we were struck with the lack of usual chatter that goes on before a church meeting. Instead, there were people sitting in pews with heads bowed, people lying prostrate on the floor weeping, and people in the back of the auditorium praying in tongues and making declarations. The startling thing was the feeling that overwhelmed us as we walked into the auditorium. The presence of the Lord was so strong and powerful that we could barely stand up.

Shortly after we were seated, a man did something we'd not seen since we left our childhood liturgical churches. The man gave a call to worship and immediately everyone came to attention. Then the man sang a short verse of scripture and the body sang the verse back to him. Then songs began to erupt from one side of the room and to our surprise, the other side answered back. Sometimes songs were spontaneous. Other times someone sang a song we knew. From every place in the room, instruments of every kind began to play—first one at a time and then multiple instruments harmonizing together. Someone played a horn that sounded like a man's voice, sort of talking, as it was being played. Later someone interpreted the sound. To our surprise, the word we heard "spoken by the horn" was the same word others heard. Wave after wave continued and with each wave came a stronger sense of the glorious presence that filled the room. A violin began to play as if a conductor has just directed the violinist to lead with a down-stroke, and a dancer stepped up on stage to interpret what the violin was playing. Next, voices from all over the auditorium began to sing in perfect harmony. A healing occurred while people continued to worship as if healings were common in their midst. For 4 or 5 hours, waves of glory continued to roll in and out until we thought something inside of us would explode if we had to experience any more of the manifest presence we'd encountered.

Everything in us resonated with the power and presence of God. We were ruined for life—something in us was transformed. Things we'd prayed about for years got resolved in those few hours, and issues we'd struggled with disappeared and have never returned. Most life-changing was the imprint that was made in our hearts and spirits. It has never left since that day. It etched the face of Jesus on our inward parts in a way that shaped our entire walk with the Lord. This encounter opened a door which led to an experience that released the Spirit of Wisdom and Revelation in our lives.

The Tabernacle of David is a lifestyle. It's an ongoing encounter with the living God. When this kind of God-encounter becomes a way of life, things in the atmosphere shift and lives are transformed forever.

God has woven understanding about the Tabernacle of David throughout the scriptures. The Tabernacle of David is God's secret weapon. As His glory is manifested in and through the church, nations will be drawn to His glory and be saved. The Tabernacle of David is the mandate God gave the Gentile church. His plan is for a progressive unveiling of revelation about the Tabernacle of David as the Gentile church matures. In Colossians 1:27, Paul said God would make known the riches of the glory of a mystery among the Gentiles—Christ in the Gentiles is the hope of glory. Matthew and Paul both make it clear that the time of the Gentiles will come to an end (see Luke 21:24; Romans 11:12 and 25). Paul declared that God would resume His dealings with the Jews as the age of the Gentiles came to a close. God's most powerful evangelism tool is the manifest presence of His Son living in the Gentiles, revealed for the entire world to see. It is clear that in addition to the Gentile nations God speaks of in Amos 9, the rebuilding of the Tabernacle of David is vitally connected to God's re-engagement with the Jews and His plan for their salvation. His Son Jesus, manifested in us, will be the transitional piece that actually unites and "makes of the two, one new man" (see Ephesians 2: 11- 19). Our connection to Israel is vital if we are to complete the work God has given the Gentiles to accomplish.

We have a significant task in front of us. It's incredible that God trusts us with this mandate. He's invited our participation and partnership. It shows what confidence He has in the Holy Spirit. He will accomplish His plans and purposes. Lord, we look forward to the time when we'll hear, "Behold, the tabernacle of God is with men, and He will dwell with them, and they will be His people, and God Himself will be with them and be their God."

CHAPTER EIGHT

ANGELIC ADMINISTRATION

Recorded throughout Scriptures, we see angels being used in God's kingdom to administrate wisdom, revelation, healing, prosperity, inheritance, deliverance, strength and skill to understand. We are also given snapshots of angelic structures in heavenly places in Colossians 1:16 which names principalities, powers, thrones and dominions.

The Book of Daniel is the first book of the Bible to name angels. Angels are called "watchers" in chapter 4. The Spirit of the Lord told me clearly that we will have more encounters with the "watchers" starting in 2010. As a matter of fact, I was told to prepare for a visitation from holy watchers.

In August 2004, Bob Jones had an encounter with a watcher. Paul Keith Davis reports that on August 12, 2004, a spiritual being appeared to Bob and identified himself as a watcher. In his thirty years of prophetic ministry, many of the Lord's messengers have spoken with Bob. However, this one possessed an overwhelming heavenly atmosphere that comes from the Lord's throne. Bob found it difficult to function in his presence. When asked why this was, the messenger responded to Bob by saying, "You are living in a new day."

Watchers function as the Lord's emissaries to fulfill His commands and to make known His counsel. They observe and record the actions of mankind and release the decrees of heaven. When God releases a decree, it causes a shift to happen in the heavens and sets events to occur on the earth. Decrees are edicts in written form. A part of the function of watchers is to help fulfill heaven's plans and agenda manifested on earth. The watchers do surveillance over all the earth. They are like the reconnaissance squad.

The angel Gabriel is first mentioned when Daniel has a vision of the ram and the goat. This is the second vision that he received. It is believed that Daniel was actually in Babylon, but transported in this vision to Shushan. Being perplexed, Daniel was trying to understand the vision (have you ever been there?). Then suddenly, there stood one having the appearance of a man and he heard a man's voice call and say, "Gabriel, make this man understand the vision."

The ram is explained to be the kings of Media and Persia (verse 20) and the goat is the king of Grecia (verse 21). Daniel is instructed by Gabriel that the overall vision is for the "time of the end." He said this twice to ensure that he understood (verse 17 and 19). It concludes with Daniel being astonished by the vision.

The next mention of Gabriel is in Daniel 9:21–27 where he gives Daniel skill to understand regarding the prophecy about the "seventy weeks." This prophecy speaks to Israel *only,* unlike the visions in chapter 2 and 7 which relate to the Gentile nations. Gabriel tells Daniel six things related to the people of Israel. The six things are (1) to finish the transgression, (2) to make an end of sins, (3) to make reconciliation for iniquity, (4) to bring in everlasting righteousness, (5) to seal up the vision and prophecy, and (6) to anoint the most holy.

When would these seventy weeks begin (verse 25)? When the decree to restore and build Jerusalem was released; that took about 100 years. It was the decree of King Artaxerxes in 444 BC (Nehemiah 2:1-8). Gabriel imparts revelation and understanding concerning future events in the kingdom of God.

Michael is first mentioned in Daniel 10:13 as one of the chief princes who came to help in this angelic confrontation. Michael's name means "Who is like God." In chapter 12:1, he stands for Israel during the time of the end. In the book of Jude, chapter 9, he is contending with the devil and then in Revelation 12:7, war broke out and Michael and his angels fought with the dragon and his angels. Michael is not recorded in scripture as saying anything to a human being. He is like the "general of heaven."

There is no doubt that the Lord of Hosts is assigning and strategically placing His hosts around the globe. He will summon legions (a Roman military term) who are ready to invade planet earth, each for the purpose of advancing the gospel of the Kingdom (Matthew 25:52–53).

Preparing to cooperate with the Lord of Hosts includes knowing our rules of engagement so we can cooperate with heaven's strategies that involve angelic assistance. Because we are seated in heavenly places (which are seats of dominion where the activities of heaven take place on earth), we are to partner and participate by our intercession and agreement with Heaven's agenda.

Along with others that rebelled with him, Lucifer (whose name meant "son of the morning") was not spared but was cast down to hell by God Himself and delivered into chains of darkness to be reserved for judgment (Isaiah 14:12-15; Jude 6 and 2Peter 2:4). According to Ephesians 6:12 there are four classes of fallen angels which are: principalities—these are of the highest rank (chief princes); powers—fallen angels who do Satan's bidding; rulers of darkness—spirit world rulers who assist with Satan's intended plans; and spiritual wickedness

<u>in the heavenly places</u>—these operate from the heavenlies which is Satan's seat of operation.

We must learn in this season how to get into alignment with the angelic so that we can be effective and efficient in the spiritual realm. Growing in spiritual discernment and sensitivity to the Holy Spirit's activities is essential to survive during these turbulent times. Learning what will hinder the assistance of angels as stated in Perry Stone's *Angels on Assignment* will help. Five things he lists are: negative speaking (Psalm 103:20); unbelief (Luke 1:13-20); sin (John 5:1-15); not giving God the glory (Acts 12:1-2, 20, 25); and disobedience (Numbers 22).

Are there enough angels for all of us? Daniel 7:9-10 and Revelation 5:11 says that there are a 'thousand thousands' that ministered to Him and 'ten thousand times ten thousand' that stood before Him (verse 10). The court was in session and the books were opened.

Chuck Missler writes that there are at least five books that will be opened at the Bema Seat of Judgment: The Book of the Living (Psalm 69:28); The Lamb's Book of Life (Revelation 3:5, 13:8); The Book of Tears (Psalm 56:8, 2Kings 20:5); The Book of Remembrance (Malachi 3:16); and the Book of Deeds (Daniel 7:10, Revelation 20:12). We pray that our eyes will be open to see and that our lives will be acceptable and pleasing to partner with the Lord of Hosts and His angelic army.

Dark forces are being strengthened and influenced by sinister spiritual beings. Principalities and hosts of wickedness are instructing militants on how to do acts of terror. The fallen angels are looking to empower those who are full of darkness to carry out Satan's agenda. In Daniel 10, we are given a pattern on how to deal with the powers of darkness. One man with a prophetic anointing prayed and fasted, and caused things to be shifted in the heavens. He was given detailed, divine revelation of world history from Darius to the time of the end of Gentile power. Imagine what a company of Emerging Daniels aligning with the angelic under the direction of the Lord of Hosts could do.

Daniel 10:11-14 gives us a glimpse of the invisible war that took place. The Prince of Persia is once again threatening Israel today. Persia today is actually Iran. President Mahmoud Ahmadinejad is leading the way to eliminate Israel. We are the ones who must rise up to take down these demonic powers. Like Daniel, we need the strong angels to come and strengthen and help us.

The following is a present day example of angelic help in the government. Chuck Ripka, international banker, entrepreneur, marketplace minister, and author of *God Out of the Box*, shares a story about how he and the ministers of Elk River, Minnesota, were assisted by angels when the destiny of their state needed to be changed. As an ambassador of the kingdom, Chuck had a specific word from God about the plans he had for bringing revival to Minnesota. However, there were spiritual bondages that needed to be broken within the state legislature. So God sent them right to the source—the state capitol building—to begin the work through prayer. Chuck says: "When we were ready to step into the Capitol, I sensed a strong demonic presence. I prayed, 'Lord would You please send warring angels to go into the Capitol before me?' Incredibly, I immediately saw two angels before me, each twenty feet tall. One had a huge hammer or mallet. They walked inside and caught a demon that looked like a Pan god from Greek mythology. It was half man and half animal. The angels bound the demon's hands, laid it on a block of granite, and then crushed its skull with the hammer. As its head was being crushed, the hand of the demon opened up and a gold key fell to the ground. The Lord said to me, 'Now with this key, no door will be locked to you.' We stepped inside and the Lord began revealing to me what He wanted done that evening."

Chuck's heart grieved because there was a separation between church and state. The Lord said that He was grieved even more because there has been a separation between church and church. Chuck and this group of ministers proceeded to pray and repent for the sins of the state and its constituents committed between racial groups, young against the old, and more. Chuck reported that their prayers and confessions had made a difference. The atmosphere had changed. There was a new spirit of cooperation within the walls of the Capitol. Following God's leading and having angelic assistance brought a shift towards righteousness.

We must learn in this season how to get in agreement and alignment with the angelic so that we can affect governments in the spiritual realm. We can see His kingdom come on earth and the gospel of the Kingdom demonstrated in every nation by releasing His decrees and partnering with His holy angels. There is a great stir in the heavens. I can hear the sound of war. Angels are declaring: *"Worthy is the Lamb who was slain, to receive power and riches and wisdom, and strength and honor and glory and blessing!"* (Revelation 5:12)

As in Daniel 10, the Prince of Persia and the Prince of Greece are once again stirring up activities against Israel. However, on the flip side there is Michael, one of the chief princes, ready and willing to respond to the commands of the Lord of Hosts.

CHAPTER NINE

MARKETPLACE INVASION

A good definition of marketplace is the community of business where most people work and spend their time. It encompasses every facet of life excluding the church. It is where the largest and greatest potential for the harvest exists. The concept of marketplace ministry is not new. The Bible notes many of them. In the Old Testament, there is Abraham, Joseph, Moses, Nehemiah, David, and Daniel. In the New Testament, the apostles were in the marketplace demonstrating the gospel of the Kingdom.

We have entered into a season of time where those who are in the business community are being called kings or builders. This invasion is the exposure to the supernatural, intangible essence of the kingdom. The Emerging Daniel Company is committed to prepare marketplace leaders with practical kingdom principles and impartations that activate the anointing for leaders to influence the culture for righteousness and the advancement of His Kingdom. Marketplace leaders can only be effective with the presence of the Spirit, the favor of God, and the supernatural empowerment of the Spirit. The presence of God will produce the tangible results needed in everyday life. The enemy fights those in the marketplace in three areas. He knows that the secret to success as kingdom builders is to spend time in the presence of the King. So he steals our time by making us too busy to take the time, then he works on destroying the covenant relationships needed to fulfill their kingdom assignment, and lastly he kills our quiet time. We are in the season where we must operate daily by the revelation of His counsel and have interceding seers like Daniel to release the counsels of heaven to those whom he was assigned. The Emerging Daniel Company is being used to bring understanding as bridge builders between ministry and marketplace, strengthening covenant relationships that advance the agenda of the Kingdom.

Kings, priests, and prophets are working together to advance the Kingdom. In the book, *Releasing the Kings*, Harold Eberle gives some attributes of biblical kings. Their mantle is having authority in the earth; their confidence is sonship and ownership; their strength is desire, vision and passion; their attitude is that they are heirs who have permission to produce; their prayer is asking whatsoever and believing; their anointing is creativity and wisdom; their mindset is that abundance is God's will, and the battle they face is breaking the poverty mentality. Those who are in the marketplace know that the greatest confrontation with the kingdom of darkness is that two systems diametrically opposed to each other presently exist. The Kingdom of God will and does take over completely (Daniel 2:44-45).

In Revelation 18 and 19, we see this final confrontation being played out in Babylon. This is where it all began. Babylon is a natural city and a spiritual analogy of Satan's kingdom on earth. Jane Hamon writes in her book, *The Cyrus Decree*, "Babylon is full of witchcraft, idolatrous practices, lust, immorality, dishonesty, greed, and evil intentions. It resists true, godly government by enforcing a false government full of man's philosophies. God has answered this resistance by raising up apostles — those who will establish God's government in the earth. Babylon loves illegitimate revelation through psychics and witchcraft. God has answered this by raising up true prophets that speak the heart, will, and mind of God. Babylon controls society through its domination in the business world, economics, and politics. God answers this control by raising up righteous men and women as ministers in the marketplace who are anointed with the favor and influence of the Holy Spirit, instructing them in the economy of the kingdom which is based on love and the "seek ye first the kingdom" principle. Acquiring a biblical worldview, they will receive His wisdom, creativity, and insight. Being anointed by the Spirit for the marketplace, they know that they are set apart and authorized by the Lord for a specific service or work. In the world of commerce they are the elders at the gates. Presently, our governmental leaders are desperately seeking solutions to the troubling economies of every nation in every continent. Now is the time that every nation needs a present day Daniel (those who can solve unsolvable problems by the wisdom of God).

The Emerging Daniel Company is forming kingdom entrepreneur seminars, assembling and having covenant relationships with coaches and mentors in the business area, developing spiritual equipping classes for marketplace men and women, and developing intercessory seers for their families and businesses. The economy of the kingdom functions through covenant alliances that together advance kingdom strategy. As the two flow as one, an inspired leadership will arise who carry the inspiration of the Holy Spirit. They are the ones destined to implement the strategies of the Lord.

KINGDOM ENTREPRENEURS: LIVING BY A KINGDOM CODE

This is the season to be creative, energetic, and innovative by the Holy Spirit. Kingdom entrepreneurs will increase in 2010. Even in the natural, this is being prophesied by the magazine *Entrepreneur* (December 2009 edition). On the front cover it says, "2010 is the Year of The Entrepreneur: Why Now is the Time to Start Something Big." We at the Emerging Daniel Company have been taking note of those whom God has been divinely aligning us with. In this section you will meet several "marketplace ministers" who are among this new generation of leaders.

Recently, I met a man named John Sipple. Jill-Marie and I were hosting a Saturday morning meeting at our home with Bob and Bonnie Jones for a small mixed group of local marketplace and ministry leaders as well as watchers and gatekeepers. It was the time the Lord appointed for us to receive the impartation of the Sons of Issachar, to understand the times, and what we needed to do. As Bob and Bonnie Jones and Jill-Marie and I started ministering to those that attended, John stood before me. I started prophesying to him about releasing and raising up those in the marketplace with the entrepreneurial spirit on them. Months later we had a breakfast meeting to get to know each other. He revealed his dreams and passions, and that he was writing a book about entrepreneurs. Here is an excerpt from John's book *What Makes an Entrepreneur?*

"*Webster* defines an entrepreneur as 'a person who organizes and manages an enterprise, especially a business, usually with considerable initiative and risk.' A leader is defined as 'one who goes before to show the way, to influence, induce or cause.' So it could be said that an entrepreneur is a leader who goes before to organize and manage an enterprise, especially a business, usually with considerable initiative and risk."

"Peter Drucker said, 'Entrepreneurs *innovate*, innovation is the specific tool of entrepreneurship.'

"A further definition from the Harvard Business School is that Entrepreneurship is *'the pursuit of opportunity beyond the resources you currently control.'* In other words, to be considered 'entrepreneurial' one must stretch beyond the current understanding and knowledge of things and into the unknown; i.e., they must think and act 'outside of the box.'

"Practically, as we look around, we see individuals who seem to be of the mold suggested by these definitions—but we don't see a lot of them. The definitions imply a high level of passion (heart) for whatever it is the individual is trying to create or change, an intuitive ability to see possibilities for innovation that others miss, and a high tolerance for uncertainty and risk; i.e., willing to take chances <u>before</u> any assurance of success.

"Such individuals seem to be rare in our present cultures of big business, big organizational thinking, rules, procedures, and a general lack of patience for the really creative person who may appear a little weird.

"But, as mentioned earlier, the landscape is different today. It's the 'Information Age' and we are seeing a return to individual thinking, the 'knowledge worker.'

"If we are made in God's image then perhaps we are to be more creative and entrepreneurial, not less. How is all of this to work? What makes one an entrepreneur—a few college courses? In light of the fact that something like 80 percent of new startup businesses fail, it seems that more must be understood than the material in a few college courses, which at best would provide some beginning knowledge and possibly some of the skills needed."

Another couple who are kingdom entrepreneurs is David and Josette Allen who share their story of how God has used them in the marketplace and for the Kingdom:

"Much like the Apostle Paul in scripture, we have worked in both the marketplace and the church deriving our income only from business in order to support the ministry. Ideas usually start with a small concept and when accomplished, take life when God breathes into it. Beginning as home renovators, we were promoted into new home development which led into hotel renovation leading to resort development, ownership and management now currently owned by Westin Resorts on St. John. But hurricane Hugo in the Virgin Islands blew us into a new business ... technology. We created and developed and patented the concept of TelePresence. TelePresence is a visual communications technology which produces big screen, life size images that has now been commercialized and deployed worldwide. God blessed this endeavor, granted favor and moved us into a capital event."

"As we were engaged in the business sector, the spiritual atmosphere was also changing. What started as a small home group became the basis of our current church, Five Rivers Vineyard located in Dayton, Ohio. Having been senior pastors for over 20 years as well as entrepreneurs has not always been an easy road to travel. There has been much misunderstanding in the Christian community regarding living life with the Bible in one hand and the briefcase in the other. Many people in the business sector as well as the church did not understand why we were doing both. Actually, in the beginning, we didn't either! But God's plans are not subject to our understanding what He is calling forth. We are simply to obey."

"After the capital event which occurred in January of 2007, our journey continued with the birthing of our current corporation, Iformata, with our headquarters located in Dayton, Ohio. Again, God inspired and downloaded creative ideas, a new set of patents and technology that, once again, is drawing the attention of many global corporations that dwarf our size. At times when obstacles seemed to rise up and hinder us, we would pray, call for heaven's strategy and even hire spiritual intercessors to help us get to the next level of growth and understanding. We understood the importance of hearing God through our dreams, prophetic words and discernment directly from God and indirectly through others."

"As our business grew, however, we knew it was not solely for the marketplace. God began a persistent calling to see how this technology would impact the spiritual realm as it was the marketplace. Large international corporations saw the need for this technology and were actively purchasing and using Iformata's services. But God never favors one over the other. Our experience has been that He uses 'all' things to advance His Kingdom. And we knew He was calling us to explore the use of this technology for His purposes."

"We had placed this technology within our church as well as our home wondering what God had in mind. It wasn't long before God made it clear. He wanted to connect up the Apostolic Centers in preparation of the shaking that was coming upon the earth. Favor and timing were released simultaneously and we started on a two year journey of following after God. The last two years have been amazing. There are now major Apostolic Centers in Hawaii, California, Washington, Illinois, Kansas City and more connected with this technology that allows greater communication, activation and preparation to propel the Kingdom into its advancement. Spiritual conferences in Washington can be piped into our church with the ability to interact with no delays in either voice or video timing. Healings have occurred in one city without the need for prayer as teaching sessions on healing were taught in Illinois. And we believe this is just the beginning!" (**Note:** *We at Emerging Daniel Company International see this Tele-Presence technology as providing the ability to connect strategic command centers that the Lord of Hosts is raising up.*)

"Not everything we've tried in business or the church has worked. There have been many 'bumps and bruises' along the way. But giving up is not really an option. As God entrusts us with His purposes, we are simply to walk them out with our limited understanding. He brings the fruit. He is moving in our hearts to get more into His Kingdom ways of thinking and doing. We feel the wind of His Spirit and know we are in a season of repositioning and transitioning. Among other endeavors, we can sense the call to bring forth a center of worship, healing and equipping using this technology. We know it's bigger than we are. That's how we know it must be God."

An amazing cluster of gift mixes are being assembled for the marketplace. Many business leaders are apostolic/prophetic and have been sent into the mountain of commerce to invade with the influence of the kingdom of God. It is the responsibility of the five-fold ministries to train and equip them to hear God, learn His ways, discern His presence, and mature in the area of spiritual warfare (Ephesians 6:10-18). They must be equipped in spiritual wisdom, understanding, and discerning of spirits, discerning the realm of the Holy Spirit, angels, the demonic, and the human spirit. They need to have the Spirit of Truth in and upon them to guide them in all truth so that they can glorify God in their kingdom assignment. To glorify God means to personally reflect His presence and to manifest His life. They will be used to provide supernatural answers and solutions to problems for which no one has answers.

Since those called to the marketplace are called builders, one of their primary purposes should be the establishing of the Tabernacles of David, creative worship centers, and Daniel academies (schools of the Spirit for the training and equipping of marketplace businessmen and women). Knowing Him must be the foundation, which is where strength, impartation, equipping, training, strategies, and understanding can be received for their families as well as their businesses. Seeking Him diligently through intimacy and communion is the order of the day. We need illumination that comes from Him who is the essence of wisdom and creativity. Creativity is a manifestation of wisdom. Biblical wisdom is the creative expression of the Holy Spirit who brings practical solutions to the issues of life.

Another couple who practices this model is Brian Kinne, a successful young marketplace minister and his wife Julie, an impassioned worshipper. Brian expresses his thoughts concerning the Sons of Issachar and its application in the marketplace.

"The Sons of Issachar, Tola, Puah, Jashub and Shimron were put in charge of over 400,000 warriors (1Chronicles 12: 23-37) all of who were more experienced, better equipped and more skilled than the Sons of Issachar. So why were these sons put in charge; given authority, responsibility and senior commandership over the army?

"1Chronicles 12:32 gives us the key to their success, "*Sons of Issachar, who understood the times and knew what Israel should do*". There are two key parts to that scripture, in that they (1) understood the times and (2) they knew what Israel should do.

"So what the Sons of Issachar did was to diligently study the role of leading a great army so that they increased in understanding and knowledge. Think of it as they did their homework and were prepared. Then, when God imparted personal understanding into them, they understood how to apply all that they had diligently learned. We can apply this biblical principle in the business world.

"As a senior executive with several global organizations, I've often found myself literally crying out to God asking him for revelation into a specific business matter I was dealing with. More times than not, I would receive a sudden word, thought or idea of which I knew had origins in Heaven. But, far too often I struggled with not understanding the word, thought or idea. I mean, it made such awesome sense (I knew I wasn't smart enough to think of it myself), but I simply didn't know how to implement it. After learning the Heavenly principles used by the Sons of Issachar, I started to apply myself 'diligently' toward my trade. I studied, was prudent with regards to my industry and learned to be cunning in the techniques I used. I also hung around as many thought leaders within my industry, hoping to gain just an ounce more of information. Eventually, I significantly increased my knowledge about my own job. The results were simply astounding. Now, when I ask for and receive 'yada,' I'm now able to 'know what to do,' which has greatly elevated me in favor with those within the business world. I am a firm believer that the principles of God's Kingdom apply to every single walk of life we find ourselves involved in."

These Kingdom principles can be applied in the world of commerce and can radically change the way in which we do business.

LEADERSHIP IN THE CRUCIBLE OF TRANSITION

Someone else who has influenced our perspective of kingdom based principles in the marketplace is Phil Zaldatte who is a life and business transitional coach. He shares his insight on leadership:

"Leadership for the most part is easy to explain, leadership is not so easy to practice. Leadership is about character and behavior first, skills second. Successful leaders are followed chiefly because people trust and respect them, rather than the skills they possess.

"Recently the Lord woke me in the night and told me, 'Son, thank you for accepting the invitation I offered you and many other leaders that I was raising up. What you and the others didn't know was that it was an invitation to the back side of the desert or wilderness to be alone with me' (Hosea 2:14-15). Another word for 'wilderness' in the Hebrew language is the word 'sanctuary'; to the Lord the wilderness is holy ground. It is an opportunity to be refined by His fiery love, to hear His voice in a fresh new way. It is in this place of feeling displaced that the Lord restores fruitfulness to us, those places that have been a stumbling block to us, we learn to overcome.

Then walk out of the wilderness with a new song in our hearts.

"In this hour God is bringing His emerging leaders into the sanctuary of transition. Churches are in transition, governments are in transition, nations are in transition, the marketplace is in transition. What got us here won't get us there; we can't get to where God has called us alone. Transformational Coaches are being called on to help leaders navigate the whitewater of change going on.

"Transition has three phases to it: First—The ending or 'Letting Go' of what was. It means letting a chapter close on old habits and behaviors that once shaped our identity. Second—The 'Neutral Zone.' The neutral zone can be compared to a wilderness experience. It is a funeral time for self images, values, attitudes and outlook. It is a time of feeling a sense of loss, and groping around for a sense of purpose and direction. The 'New beginning' is not yet in focus but you know a new day has dawned and there is no going back. Third—'The New Beginning.' It is usually marked by a release of new energy in a new direction; they are the expression of a new identity. Beginnings involve new understandings, new values, new attitudes and most of all—new identities.

"The Bible has many examples of these three phases of transition. A good example of the first phase or 'The ending' was in the book of Joshua chapter one. We see Joshua being told by the Lord, 'My servant Moses is dead.' Now it was time for him to go from servant to Moses to now being the leader. One season had ended and now it was time to begin heading to the Promised Land. They couldn't see it yet but they knew it was coming.

"The second phase was their time of preparation in the wilderness before crossing the Jordan. Chapter 3, verse 5, consecrating themselves—setting themselves apart to get ready to embrace the new beginning.

"The third phase we can see in the crossing over the Jordan in chapter 3. The Jordan is symbolic of crossing over from death into life. As we are stepping into our own Promised Land blessing or ascending our own cultural mountain, what are we modeling to the world?

"In 3rd John verse 2, it says, *'Beloved, I pray that you may Prosper in All Things and be in Health, just as your soul prospers.* It is God's will that we prosper in five specific areas:

1-Spiritually
2-Emotionally
3-Physically
4-Financially
5-Relationally

"It was said of Daniel he had a Spirit of excellence in all that he did. I believe that as God's kids prosper in all five of these areas we will catch the attention of the world. It says in Isaiah chapter 60, *"Arise and shine; For your light has come! And the Glory of the Lord is risen upon you. For behold, the darkness shall cover the earth, and deep darkness the people: But the Lord shall arise over you, And His Glory will be seen upon you. The Gentiles shall come to your light, and kings to the brightness of your rising."*

"The need for skilled and anointed coaches will intensify in the coming days as the Lord transitions His emerging champions in these five areas of life. The 'Deep Darkness' coming upon people and nations in Isaiah 60 speaks of people and nations groping around blindly searching for solutions or answers for personal and national problems. God's Daniels, Josephs and Esthers will emerge with solutions and vision.

"Apostolic Coaches are about to come on the world scene planting 'Dream Centers' or 'Idea Labs for success.' These centers will be incubators for an emerging generation of culture shapers/coaches for the coming outpouring of the Kingdom of God. We are about to invade the 9 to 5 Window in such a way that will be historic. The Marketplace Invasion that has been prophesied about is about to take place. Revelation 11:15 says, 'The Kingdoms of this world shall become the Kingdoms of our Lord and His Christ.' These 'Incubators' will be the training centers for the Daniels, Josephs and Esthers who will invade these kingdoms in the coming days."

In the book, *The Joseph-Daniel Calling,* Morris E. Ruddick (pages 23–24), states that the kingdom operates on the premise that there is a unique difference between a kingdom executive, an official, entrepreneur, or business owner with a call to accomplish God's perspective with a kingdom agenda.

The marketplace will be the context for the majority of the wealth transfer. Understanding the extent of the wealth transfer will require an understanding of God's economy. It is said that the transference of wealth will happen when the church realizes that God's vehicle for this transfer is business. Business people in the kingdom will be given witty ideas and creative insights through dreams and visions. The silver and gold belongs to the Lord of the harvest, the shaking has begun, and the wealth will be transferred. *"The silver is mine and the gold is mine,"* says the Lord. *"The glory of this latter temple shall be greater than the former, says the Lord of Hosts. And in this place I will give peace,' says the Lord of Hosts"* (Haggai 2:8-9).

CHAPTER TEN

STEWARDING MYSTERIES

On May 30, 2005, my friend and colleague Carolyn Blunk suddenly passed away. It was a bittersweet time; we knew she went to be with Jesus, but all of us at Streams Ministries missed her dearly. Carolyn had been John Paul Jackson's editor and publishing manager for years, long before John Paul moved his office from Texas to New Hampshire. She had helped him craft several books, a magazine, and countless articles. She was tireless in her encouragement of emerging authors like myself, Shawn Bolz, and others.

Before she died, she had read an article Shawn had submitted to the Elijah List. In it, he had mentioned something about Daniel. When she saw it in her e-mail, Carolyn picked up the phone and called him.

"Shawn," she said, "while I was reading the article, I heard the Lord tell me that you are going to have an encounter with Daniel."

Shawn and Carolyn were very close. In fact, he would often call her "Auntie Carolyn" as a term of affection for the role she played in his life and writing. Shortly after she passed away, Shawn had a dream where he was walking in heavenly places.

In the dream, Shawn came upon a round table where Carolyn was sitting with some men. Excited to see her,

Shawn ran to her and shouted her name: "Carolyn! Carolyn!" Carolyn looked at him, smiled, patted his hand, and gestured toward a man at the table.

"Shawn," she said, "I want you to meet someone. Meet Daniel," she said.

Daniel looked at Shawn and said, "It's Daniel 2:22." The dream ended.

Heaven wants the Daniel Company to steward something special, something that has been hidden away in the kingdom until now. Daniel 2:22 confirms this: *"He reveals deep and secret things; He knows what is in the darkness, and light dwells with Him."*

When I heard about this encounter, my heart jumped. I want to be part of this generation, this company of people who do whatever it takes to be friends of God. Because Daniel was dearly beloved, God opened the mysteries of the ages to him and allowed him to see into the heavenly realms. Prophetic visions and angelic visitations take time to acquire and come with a cost. But Daniel was willing to pay the price, and so should we, simply because we love Him and long for more of Him in our lives.

A Biblical mystery is a truth that is veiled until its appointed time to be revealed. Mysteries are prophetic proclamations of His purpose. In Revelation 10:1-11, a strong angel had a little book open in his hand, he cries with a loud voice as when a lion roars. Seven thunders utter their voices, John the revelator is about to write what he hears but a voice from Heaven instructs him to seal up the things which the seven thunders uttered. The angel raised up his hand to heaven and proclaims that in the days of the sounding of the seventh angel that the mystery of God would be finished.

In Revelation 11:15 the seventh angel sounded and there were loud voices in heaven saying, "The kingdoms of this world have become the kingdoms of our Lord and Christ and He shall reign forever and ever." The little book seems to be connected to the book first mentioned in Daniel 12:4 and Revelation 5:1-2. To eat the book is to have experiential knowledge. The book was sealed in Daniel's time and kept in the right hand of the Father. Prophetically, we can declare that the open book and its content (mysteries) are available to us today.

PREPARED FOR A VISITATION

Daniel's years of faithfulness and devotion to the Lord gave him the capacity to handle visitations that other men simply couldn't bear. In Daniel 10:7, we read that only the prophet himself could discern what God was doing: *"I, Daniel, alone saw the vision, for the men who were with me did not see the vision; but a great terror fell upon them, so that they fled to hide themselves."* While others ran away in fear, Daniel experienced an amazing visitation:

> *I lifted my eyes and looked, and behold, a certain man clothed in linen, whose waist was girded with gold of Uphaz!*
>
> *His body was like beryl, his face like the appearance of lightning, his eyes like torches of fire, his arms and feet like burnished bronze in color, and the sound of his words like the voice of a multitude* (Daniel 10:5-6).

Daniel 10 tells us that it took three touches from the angel to give Daniel the strength to stand in his presence. Only then was he able to receive understanding for what he had been seeing. He had proven himself worthy to heaven.

The Emerging Daniel Company can have that same capacity by living in the three things we've been talking about: unity, intimacy, and maturity. In this vision, Daniel was given insight into a conflict that has lasted twenty-five-hundred years: Iran versus Iraq. Nothing has changed since his day.

Even more startling is the Daniel 11 revelation of the antichrist. Daniel 11:1-35 describes the major rulers of the Persian Empire and then gives in great detail some of the major events of the third empire following Alexander the Great, concluding with Antiochus Epiphanes. Verses 36 through 45 deals with the last Gentile ruler who will be in power when the Lord Jesus returns. No wonder the enemy had tried to kill Daniel so many times; he did not want his master plan released. Thanks to Daniel's devotion and revelation, intercessors throughout the ages know the blueprint of the enemy's end-times plan. We can pray with wisdom, insight, and understanding. We can persevere, knowing victory is on its way. In short, this vision gives saints the finishing faith.

NOW IS THE TIME

We live in the most exciting time in human history. The activity of heaven has been shifted into another gear. In recent years, we have seen many confirming prophetic words given. Most of us who walk in the revelatory realm have had this happen—we have received a prophetic word that confirmed something that was previously given. In this book, I have included several confirming words relating to the Emerging Daniel Company. Some mature vessels have even had new or future words, which are usually confirmed through other people.

Something is changing in heaven. Christians are receiving more "now" words from the Lord than ever before. Put simply, now words are being revealed and occurring immediately. What used to take ten years to come to fruition now takes days. As heaven shifts, God is declaring a new way of doing things. We see this pattern happen in Ezekiel 12:21–28:

And the word of the LORD came to me, saying,

"Son of man, what is this proverb that your people have about the land of Israel, which says: The days are prolonged, and every vision fails?"

Tell them therefore, "Thus says the Lord God: I will lay this proverb to rest, and they shall no more use it as a proverb in Israel." But say to them, "The days are at hand, and the fulfillment of every vision.

For I am the LORD. I speak, and the word which I speak will come to pass; it will no more be postponed; for in your days O rebellious house, I will say the word and perform it: says the Lord God."

Again the word of the LORD came to me saying,

"Son of man, look, the house of Israel is saying: The vision that he sees if for many days from now, and he prophesies of times far off.

Therefore say to them, "Thus says the Lord GOD: None of My words will be postponed any more, but the word which I speak will be done, says the Lord God."

Many Christians are coming to a place of consecration where we can be trusted with now words. Around the world, God is giving now words to churches, cities, regions, people groups, and even nations. As soon as these now words are declared, things begin to happen. This is the season we live in. What we do with it is up to us. Will we receive these words, ask for insight, and carry God's work forward? Or will we squander one of the most important seasons in human history?

God is forming the Emerging Daniel Company to see His kingdom proclaimed at all costs. We live in unity with one another, in intimacy with God, and in maturity in our circumstances. This Company cannot be stopped, for God is with us. Will you step forward, shining like a star, and point the way to the brightest Light of them all?

THE REVEALER OF SECRETS

The Revealer of Secrets is still active and operative in the affairs of men. Job 12:22 says: *He uncovers deep things out of darkness.* In 1Corinthians 2:10, Paul states that "God reveals to us through His Spirit for the Spirit searches all things, yes the deep things of God."

A mature company of believers will be stewarding the deep things of God as the Spirit searches all things. The Lord is looking for those He can reveal and trust with His secrets. In Ezekiel 28:1-5, the lamentation to the Prince of Tyre from the Lord says in verse 3, *"Behold! You are wiser than Daniel! There is no secret that can be hidden from you!"* There is only one revealer of secrets: Daniel 2:22.

CHAPTER ELEVEN

APOSTOLIC GOVERNMENT

The reformers are coming! The reformers are coming! Actually they are already here! In the last two years, we have seen unprecedented change in the political and financial arenas. Everything that can be shaken is currently being shaken.

The Book of Haggai foretold of a time and season where shaking would occur. Seven spheres of life are being shaken.

1. The heavens—the sky, weather patterns, atmosphere
2. The earth—volcanoes, earthquakes
3. The sea—tsunamis, tidal waves
4. The dry land—vegetation and plant life
5. All nations—national and social infrastructures
6. Religion—multitudes coming to the desire of all nations
7. Economic disruption—God transferring wealth (Haggai 2:6–8).

What is actually happening with all this shaking? What is this apostolic reformation producing? Daniel Chapter 2 tells us about a stone that is growing into a mountain. It is the Kingdom of God taking over, transforming present conditions. The Lord of loving-kindness is making a statement that His kingdom rules over all and that its influence of justice and righteousness cannot co-exist with the kingdom of men. The Lord of Hosts is reclaiming the earth for His kingdom, creating a culture that reflects His values and establishing communities that perpetuate His life and light. The glory of the King will cover the earth as the waters cover the seas.

This apostolic reformation is being carried out by the power of the Spirit and the counsel of the Lord. The Spirit of Counsel and Might will be displayed like never before. The Lord of Hosts, which is mentioned over 240 times in the Bible, is arising. A corporate shifting in the way we think and respond to the purposes of heaven is needed in this hour. Spiritual leaders are being trained and equipped for the purpose of establishing the sovereignty of God. The government of God is His wisdom and His ways are being administrated. Seeing things His way, following and applying them in this season, is non-negotiable. Isaiah 28:29 states, *"This also is from the Lord of Hosts, Who is wonderful in counsel and excellent in guidance."*

Hebrews 12:1 describes a great cloud of witnesses that surround us.

> *Therefore since we also are surrounded with so great a cloud of witnesses, let us lay aside every weight and the sin which so easily besets us, and let us run with patience the race that is set before us.*

The writer of Hebrews assumes the end-time purposes of God will be fulfilled and the race will be won by a generation that understands and builds on the victories purchased by saints who have paid the price and laid down their lives—the cloud of witnesses that has gone before us. These forerunners paid the price to pave the way for the conclusion of the ages that will be realized in our day, through an apostolic reformation.

We have arrived at the place where the only thing that can stop the downward spiral is an outpouring of the Spirit. Humanism, philosophy, political activism and religion all have failed. The Lord of Hosts is raising up an Apostolic government. One main purpose of the government of God is for the transformation and maturity of the Body of Christ—sons and daughters who experience the reality of the Kingdom of God.

The Apostolic will be activating and releasing the anointing that is already present in the believer but not yet manifested by awakening the reality that the Kingdom of God within us has the greatness of His power available. This government of mature men and women of God is here for the express purpose of helping to access spiritual inheritance and prophetic destiny. They are those who have spiritual discernment concerning the "Four Winds of Heaven" (Daniel 7:2, Daniel 8:8, Daniel 11:4). The Four Winds of Heaven signify heavenly powers of God setting in motion the earthly realms.

They will be raising up those who are assigned to promote the gospel of the Kingdom to the nations and to strengthen and equip those who are called to occupy the "high places." A quote about the high places from the movie *Lions for Lambs* defines the purpose of a high place: "Taking the high ground is the key. Whoever takes it has the ability to observe [*watchers*], the prerogative to attack [*spiritual warfare*] and the opportunity to preside" [*establish the Kingdom or establish His presence*].

Knowing our divine assignment will empower us to walk with God in this season. Also, being in divine alliance will cause us to access our destinies. Alliance is defined as a formal agreement that establishes a relationship or partnership between two or more parties to achieve a particular goal. An alliance is a treaty of friendship that has common goals and interests. Divine alliances produce spheres of safety. In an alliance you keep your own identity while being in agreement to a cause with others (1Samuel 20:12). We can only appropriate our prophetic destinies by being led by His Spirit and speaking His word in every situation. Like Daniel, we must be committed to God's kingdom and His righteousness.

This generation, this Emerging Daniel Company, that God is establishing is contending for two things: We are fighting for our inheritance—unclaimed promises of the past—and for the next righteous generation—promises of the future. Daniel received wisdom for his own circumstances, *and* he was given deep insight into the challenges future servants of God would face. Armed with these tools, this company of people are called to recognize, raise, and release until the fullness of the Gentiles comes in (Romans 11:25).

REFORMING FOUNDATIONS

Apostolic Reformation is about reforming foundations. As wise master builders like Paul, we realize that we are in an invisible war. We need to know the rules of engagement and our measure of rule (which are the limits of the sphere God appoints for us — 2Corinthians 10:13). We need to know and grow in spiritual authority and maturity, thinking strategically, relying on our Captain, the Lord of Hosts, to direct and lead us to secure our inheritances. Together we must inquire of Him to receive the manifold wisdom of God (Ephesians 3:10), which is a display of His Creative Genius.

The Daniels will have the governmental anointing that helps administrate the amazing gift-mixes that will actually reform nations. Reformation involves discipling nations. We are called to teach all nations.

We see the need for an increase in governmental intercession. The Lord is laying His burden for the nations on us. Things are still hanging in the balance. As the shaking and shifting continues in the nations, the Kingdom of God is being established. The stone is turning into a mountain. The Kingdom of God is designed to take over, not to co-exist.

Forerunners are declaring, "Prepare the Ark of the Lord." They have the "now"" word of proclamation, emphasizing what the Spirit is saying and doing. Their declarations are bringing new understanding to all the activity taking place, helping people to not be deceived or lose heart.

This Apostolic Reformation is changing the way apostles and prophets have been used, no longer just emphasizing the ecclesiastical realm. Now the Lord of light is releasing apostles and prophets in economics, technology, science, government, businesses, the military, and the arts. This is not the first time God has done this. Moses, being a prophet, administrated the social, political, economic, and military systems of Israel. Joseph's prophetic anointing was used through his office of prime minister that involved economics, management, and resources. Nehemiah, in rebuilding the wall of Jerusalem, functioned as a master builder. His anointing covered the religious, social, economic, and political arenas. The list goes on as He uses His people to reform and invade.

The Apostle Paul, a master builder, was responsible for touching over twelve influential people. Acts 13 through Acts 25 cover a political ruler, chief leaders in Asia, an entrepreneur, religious leaders, two governors, a king and Caesar. One of the purposes for this apostolic grace is to place every believer in their assigned place and to help form a new leadership for His purposes, seeing into the future, and bringing them into their giftedness. Church as usual is over—Thy kingdom come means a commitment to aligning with everything that pertains to the coming of His kingdom.

FERTILE MISSION FIELDS IN AMERICA

It was amazing to me to learn there are 101 ethnic groups in America, each needing to encounter His presence. Imagine if just one from each family of the people groups represented here were to experience the presence of the Lord and in turn touch others in their family who may still be all over the world! Check this out:

Acadians, African-Americans, Albanian-Americans, Amish, Apaches, Arab-Americans, Argentinean-Americans, Armenian-Americans, Australian and New Zealander-Americans, Austrian Americans, Barbadian Americans, Belarusian Americans, Belgian Americans, Brazilian Americans, Bulgarian Americans, Cambodian Americans, Canadian Americans, Carpatho-Rusyn Americans, Chaldean Americans, Cherokees, Chilean Americans, Chinese Americans, Choctaws, Colombian Americans, Costa Rican Americans, Creeks, Creoles, Croatian Americans, Cuban Americans, Czech Americans, Danish Americans, Dominican Americans, Dutch Americans, Ecuadoran Americans, Egyptian Americans, English Americans, Filipino Americans, French Americans, French-Canadian Americans, German Americans, Greek Americans, Guatemalan Americans, Guyanese Americans, Gypsy Americans, Haitian Americans, Hawaiians, Hmong Americans, Honduran Americans, Hungarian Americans, Indonesian Americans, Iranian Americans, Irish Americans, Iroquois Confederacy, Italian Americans, Jamaican Americans, Japanese Americans, Jewish Americans, Korean Americans, Laotian Americans, Latvian Americans, Lithuanian Americans, Maltese Americans, Mexican Americans, Mormons, Navajos, Nicaraguan Americans, Nigerian Americans, Norwegian Americans, Ojibwa, Pakistani Americans,

Palestinian Americans, Panamanian Americans, Peruvian Americans, Polish Americans, Portuguese Americans, Pueblos, Puerto Rican Americans, Romanian Americans, Russian Americans, Salvadoran Americans, Samoan Americans, Scottish and Scotch-Irish Americans, Serbian Americans, Sioux, Slovak Americans, Slovenian Americans, Spanish Americans, Swedish Americans, Swiss Americans, Syrian-Lebanese Americans, Thai Americans, Tlingit, Trinidadian and Tobagonian Americans, Turkish Americans, Ukrainian Americans, Vietnamese Americans, Welsh Americans, and Yupiat.

We believe that out of each of these people groups, Daniels will emerge to carry the message of the kingdom. We are looking for those places where all the tribes worship together. As we move toward the greatest release of apostolic authority and power ever experienced by God's sons and daughters, the rebuilding of the Tabernacle of David is foundational to the building of God's kingdom and the establishing of His authority.

CHAPTER TWELVE

TRANSITIONAL GENERATION

This transitional generation, which will be trans-generational and multi-ethnic, will arise and cross over into their inheritance. Joshua was instructed to *"arise and enter into the land of promise"* (Joshua 1:1-2). In the fullness of time, there will be a kingdom people who have cooperated with the Lord concerning His purpose and the process. A generation of overcomers that bear His image and Christ-likeness are destined to participate as the "warrior bride" with the Lord of Hosts, reclaiming, re-gathering, and restoring all things (Acts 3:21). Every "nation, tribe and tongue" is invited to advance His kingdom and deliver unto the Lord His reward (Psalm 2:8).

Through this *transitional generation*, the outpouring of the Spirit in its fullness will release the manifestation and demonstration of mantles, bloodline gifts, and blessings. Spiritual and natural inheritances will be released from the Heavenly Trust Fund account! Daniel 12:13 gives us a perspective for those who contend and remain loyal to the Lord. *"But you, (Daniel), go your way until the end. For you shall rest and will arise to your inheritance at the end of the days."*

TWO KINDS OF INHERITANCE

In Galatians 4:6-7 we see that the Spirit of His Son entering our hearts brings us into adoption (the Family of God). Abba Father receives us as sons and daughters and we are made heirs of God through Christ. Heirs of God's inheritance are given to all that receive the testimony that God sent His Son. *"as many as receive Him, to them He gives the right to become children of God, to those who believe in His name"* (John 1:12).

The second inheritance is what Daniel was told to wait for and what you and I are counseled to strive for. It is called the 'inheritance *from* the Lord' (Strong's 2817) (kleronoma). This is given by the Lord to those who are faithful, obedient and persevere. Colossians 3:24 states, *"knowing that from the Lord you will receive the reward of the inheritance for you serve the Lord Christ."*

We must inherit the Kingdom. Our lifestyle will determine the positions, rewards and authority given to us at the bema seat of Christ (1Corinthinan 3:11-15).

1Peter 1:3-5 confirms that there is an inheritance reserved in heaven for us (verse 4) and the timeline is in verse 5, ready to be revealed in the end times. What qualifies us for this inheritance? In 1Peter 1:6-16, it reveals a lifestyle that not only prepares us for the final prize but empowers us to navigate these turbulent times.

CASTING OUR CROWNS

According to Scripture the rewards or crowns we receive are defined by the levels of authority and/or responsibilities that we will receive from the Lord. There are five crowns mentioned in scripture:

The Incorruptible Crown: also called the "victor's" crown and is awarded for self-control and having victory over the flesh (1Corinthians 9:24-25).

The Crown of Rejoicing: awarded for fruitful labor for the Lord in the lives of others (1Thessolonians 2:19).

The Crown of Life: for those who have persevered, endured trials, and even faced death and yet still remained faithful (James 1:12; Revelation 2:10).

The Crown of Glory: for those who have shepherded and tended the flock and yearned to see them grow. These have the heart of Christ (1Peter 5:4).

The Crown of Righteousness: those who radiate Christ's life in all they do (2 Timothy 4:8). They live His life, do His will and love His appearing.

The Lord once spoke to me by an inner audible voice saying that it really comes down to worship and economics. Jesus was tempted by the devil (Matthew 4:8-10) with kingdoms, glory, and things. In this season, it will be clear whose kingdom we are promoting and advancing and who is being glorified. Watching and guarding our hearts from deception, which was the first strategy of the enemy, will be the number one spirit release during these times (Matthew 24:4, 11). We must access the counsel of the Lord, which is faithfulness and truth (Isaiah 25:1). Divine counsel and the wisdom from above are desperately needed in this hour of human history.

Unity, holy allegiances, and every member of the body of Christ moving in agreement and alignment will manifest His glory in the midst of a crooked and perverse generation. This is the Lord's Prayer that will be answered in this transitional generation (John 17:21-25). Only the Spirit of the Lord with divine counsel can pull this off. As we, individually and corporately, establish lifestyles of encountering Him, we can guard our hearts, which will allow us to see how to dismantle the schemes of the evil one.

There is an overcoming company of people arising. The emerging Daniels are harvesters of the great harvest. Being empowered by the seven Spirits of God, they are transformed and matured to walk in the fullness of His purpose. Daniel encountered one from heaven who had a seven-fold description as *"being dressed in linen, with a belt made of gold, a body like beryl (transparent gemstone), arms like glowing bronze, a face like lightning, eyes like fire and a strong voice"* (Daniel 10:5-6). So shall this company encounter and receive help from on high to live victorious in the transitional generation.

The following is a dream experience which occurred on August 23, 2007 as described by Jill-Marie:

> *The actual dream was in three separate segments—the first two pertain to other matters. The third visionary frame of the dream opens wherein I was in what appears to be a hospital delivery room. I was in bed in the birthing position; Aaron was standing at the foot of the bed working with a black laptop computer. It appears we are waiting— one of the things I noticed in the dream was that I was not "laboring" at this time. After seeing Aaron, I turned my head to the left and saw four baby strollers with babies who all appeared to be the same size, but I "knew" they were not all the same age. Their head/faces seemed larger than their bodies, but two prominent features that caught my attention: large eyes and very deep dimples! As I am looking at the babies in the dream, it was as if my thoughts were aloud because the baby in the stroller, second from the right, leans over to speak to the baby in the first stroller on the left and said, "She likes our dimples!" I was amused that "they" knew what I had been thinking and turned to look back at Aaron. When I did, I saw that someone else was standing with him, a man who was one of my former employers—also with a laptop, but his was smaller and was silver in color. He was showing something to Aaron. The dream then ended. When I awoke in the morning, I told Aaron I had had this "strange" dream and he said*

to share it with him anyway. (It is interesting that what we think is odd, when you start to process, it starts to make sense.).

The first part is pretty easy—Aaron and I were obviously getting ready to birth something. What is interesting is the significance of the man that joined Aaron at the foot of the bed. When I worked with this man, the company specialized in mechanical design and facilities engineering. One of the services we provided was called "commissioning." (In the industry, basically, commissioning is referred to as a systematic process that will ensure that all mechanical systems and components will interact and operate in accordance with each other to deliver the desired "atmospheric" conditions for the use of the space they are serving. Obviously, the needs for a surgical room space differ from those in, say, a warehouse environment.) The next noteworthy fact is that the man's name is Howard, but he was known in the industry as "Howie"—I laughed at God's sense of humor as it appears that what he was showing to Aaron was "how we" will do this—that which we are being commissioned for. Beyond this, I was unclear on the significance of the four babies and just recorded what I knew then.

Interestingly, this dream occurred just before Aaron and I were about to minister at Gateway Church in West Haven, Connecticut with Bob and Bonnie Jones, Shawn Bolz, and Paul Keith Davis for a gathering called "When the Glory Came Down." At one of the meetings after Shawn had gotten through speaking, he called Aaron and me over to the side of the platform and said he had a personal question to ask. He asked if we were "pregnant" along with some other personal words. He said he felt like we were being commissioned for something. Now we had not mentioned this dream to those at the conference. Then Paul Keith Davis came over and said he saw that a cloak was resting upon us to be empowered with authority.

Some months later, I had yet another dream wherein among other things shown unto me, the Lord appeared and told me He was going to give me further insight to this prior dream because I had often pondered the significance of the babies in the strollers. The Lord told me that they represented four prior movements of His glory and that while they were "pleasing to the eye," so to speak, these movements had not ever grown beyond a certain stage to maturity (which is why to me they looked similar, but sensed they were of different ages). The Lord went on to say that there is a fifth baby about to be born (meaning to me that a <u>new expression of His glory</u> is about to be released) and that "how it" or "how we" will be released is through the use of technology. In the dream, I was thinking of media as the means. Again, reading my thoughts, the Lord said, "No, that is too limiting of a vision." (Upon further researching the definition of technology, I found it deals with usage and knowledge of tools and crafts, and how it affects one's ability to control and adapt to its environment.) I understand now how this relates to the Emerging Daniel Company in our vision for advancing the kingdom through the marketplace. It will be through the knowledge and use of individual gifts or talents or crafts affecting their sphere of influence—outside of the church environment.

In wanting to gain further insight into the natural birthing process, I found that there are stages of labor. A parallel can be seen here because that which is true in the natural applies in spiritual matters (on earth as it is in heaven).

In the first stage there are actually three sub-phases and is what most people identify as labor. Stage One consists of early labor, active labor and transition. Stage Two is the pushing stage, and Stage Three is the actual birth.

Early labor is described as the initial phase that can last hours, days or even weeks. It can be characterized by excitement (Can we possibly see the relation to the initial excitement we feel when we receive understanding from the Lord of our calling? We make plans and get ready—then, it happens—distractions, discouragement, and disillusionment creep in—the wind gets knocked out of us—contractions.)

Active labor is when birthing becomes more serious—with each contraction, relaxation and breathing become very important. Tuning out distraction and creating a positive environment will be important.

Transition is by far the most challenging, although the shortest, phase of birthing. This is when you might begin to feel overwhelmed and your focus might falter. This is the phase usually depicted in the media. Transition is the storm before the calm that is pushing. It is by far the hardest part of birthing, but also the shortest. This is the stage where you may doubt your ability to birth your baby. You may feel worried about how far you have left to go and how much more intense it will become. You will be suggestible and at this time are most vulnerable to accepting interventions whether they will be helpful or not.

The pushing stage, the second phase of labor, will end with the much-anticipated birth of the baby. This is probably the most empowering part of the experience and can be the most motivating and comfortable. Pushing is usually much more manageable than transition. You will feel your body pushing independent of any extra effort on your part. Remember, this is exactly what is supposed to happen. (excerpt from: www.givingbirth-naturally.com/stages-of-labor)

Rest is our greatest weapon in these transitional times. The rest of God is a place as well as an experience. It has two applications. For our present circumstances, it means resting in the finished work of Christ. In other words, allowing Him to live His life out through us. Its future application is participating in the millennium with Christ, having completed the warfare and overcoming what was set before us (Hebrews 4; Matthew 11:28-29). Transitional leaders will join the generations so that the fullness of the expression of the kingdom can be demonstrated to the world. They will flow into advisory capacity.

We are transitioning from a shakable kingdom to an unshakable kingdom. We are being transformed from a weak and irrelevant church to a glorious church. The glorious church has the manifested visible and tangible presence of the Lord. We are transitioning into mature sons and daughters of God who carry the fullness of the Spirit and who walk with God. A whole generation of Daniels is about to emerge.

FINISHING STRONG

How can we finish strong during this transitional season? The answers are in Daniel chapters 10-12. Daniel was strengthened by fasting and praying (Daniel 10:12 *Because you set your heart* was used by the angel). He received supernatural strength by the revelation that he was greatly beloved (Daniel 10:11, 19). He was touched and strengthened by an angel on three separate occasions (Daniel 10:10, 16, 18). Finally, he was given divine understanding (Daniel 10:11, 14).

Like Daniel, we will be strengthened by fasting and prayer, by receiving the revelation that we are greatly beloved and by being assisted by the angelic realm in receiving the spirit of understanding (Daniel 12:10 — *Many shall be purified, made white and refined, but the wicked shall do wickedly. And none of the wicked shall understand, but the wise shall understand*).

The Emerging Daniel Company, International is a multi-ethnic, multi-generational company of individuals who have developed and matured in their gifting and calling with the skill, anointing and understanding to prepare for the times and seasons we are in known as Kingdom consultants. Their purpose is to equip, strengthen and activate leadership in specific arenas of life to align with Kingdom principles through gatherings, seminars, training sessions and consultations.

**THE EMERGING DANIEL COMPANY
INTERNATIONAL
P.O. BOX 268
BOXFORD, MA 01921
www.emergingdanielcompany.com**